Faith, Values and Sex & Relationships Education

Simon Blake and Zarine Katrak

SEX EDUCATION FORUM

The Sex Education Forum

The Sex Education Forum is the national authority on sex and relationships education (SRE). We believe that good quality SRE is an entitlement for all children and young people. We are working with our 49 member organisations to achieve this.

If you work with young people, in school or in a youth or community setting as a teacher, health professional, social worker or you are a parent or carer we can help provide you with the information and support you need to provide effective sex education. We work with teachers and health professional across all settings promoting good practice through a range of publications and factsheets. If you have a query or need more information about any aspect of SRE you can call our information helpline on 020 7843 6052 or e-mail us at sexedforum@ncb.org.uk or visit www.ncb.org.uk/sef.

The National Children's Bureau

The National Children's Bureau promotes the interests and well-being of all children and young people across every aspect of their lives. NCB advocates the participation of children and young people in all matters affecting them. NCB challenges disadvantage in childhood.

NCB achieves its mission by
◆ ensuring the views of children and young people are listened to and taken into account at all times
◆ playing an active role in policy development and advocacy
◆ undertaking high quality research and work from an evidence based perspective
◆ promoting multidisciplinary, cross-agency partnerships
◆ identifying, developing and promoting good practice
◆ disseminating information to professionals, policy makers, parents and children and young people.

NCB has adopted and works within the UN Convention on the Rights of the Child.

Published by National Children's Bureau Enterprises Ltd, the trading company for the National Children's Bureau, Registered Charity number 258825, 8 Wakley Street, London EC1V 7QE. Tel: 020 7843 6000

© National Children's Bureau, 2002
Published 2002

ISBN 1 900990 32 6

British Library Cataloguing in Publication Data
A catalogue record for this book is available from the British Library

Designed and typeset by Jeff Teader
Printed and bound by Page Bros, Norwich

Contents

Acknowledgements

This resource is the result of a large number of individuals who have worked together to explore the issues and offer positive strategies for ensuring effective sex and relationships education. Thank you to all of the young people, community members and professionals who attended meetings and consultation events. There are too many of you to name individually, but we hope we have managed to capture your perspectives. The following people have all made particularly generous contributions by organising and attending meetings, grappling with complex issues and reading draft(s) of the resource.

Jane Armstrong
Khalida Ashrafi
Jeffrey Blumenfeld
Annie Blunt
Geoff Brown
Rose Brown
Helen Chambers
Mille Clare
Diane Coke
Liz Ellerton
David Fitch
Gill Frances
Mark Halstead
Mark Hankinson

David Herbert Tarvin
Jeanette Herbert Tarvin
Lynne Hutchinson
David Lankshear
Mary Lanovy-Taylor
Andrea Mason
Marilyn Mason
Paul Mattis
Nazar-E-Mustafa
Varsha Patel
Hansa Patel-Kanwal
Martin Pendergast
Stephanie Quiggley
Caroline Ray

Michael Reiss
Caroline Riley
Manjit S Rooprah
June Sanderson
Parminder Sekhon
Janet Sheehan
Derek Simmonds
Gulab Singh
David Stevinson
John Swallow
Cyril Sweeney
Meena Temple
Karen Turner
Kathleen Wood

A special thanks to all the children and young people who always talked so freely about sex and relationships education and values to assist us in this challenging piece of work. Thanks to Jane Hobden for editing the resource so well, to Helen Chenaf and Tracy Anderson for administrative support and finally thanks to the Teenage Pregnancy Unit at the Department of Health for funding its production.

Introduction

Why SRE needs a multi-faith perspective

Children and young people from all faiths and cultures have an entitlement to sex and relationships education (SRE) that supports them on their journey through childhood to adolescence and adulthood. One young woman, aged 15, emphasised the importance of receiving this entitlement.

> **'I have a faith and I trust my parents to talk to me about values. At school what I need in sex education is to understand about sex and relationships and understand what different people think.'**

It is this expressed need from children and young people to know and understand about sex, sexuality and relationships, alongside our public health concerns such as teenage pregnancy, HIV and sexually transmitted infections, that makes it imperative that effective SRE is developed within schools and other settings.

Teaching effective SRE means taking into account the many faiths and cultures of the children and young people in Britain today. In its Sex and Relationship Education Guidance (DfEE 2000) the Department for Education and Employment emphasises that SRE should be sensitive to the range of different values and beliefs within a multi-faith and multi-cultural society (DfEE, 2000, page 12). It goes on to stress the importance of SRE being developed in partnership with parents/carers and the wider community (page 12).

While most educators, young people, parents and carers support SRE, it causes anxiety and concern for many. The confidence of those delivering SRE is often undermined by assumptions and stereotypes about how the subject is taught. They are also unclear about which values should be promoted, and have worries about a lack of parental support.

The Forum and multi-faith work

The Sex Education Forum represents over 50 organisations including religious, children's, parent and governor, health, education and specialist organisations. All member organisations are committed to securing the entitlement of children and young people to effective sex and relationships education. Since the inception of the Sex Education Forum, many of its members have:

◆ worked with and challenged assumptions about sex and relationships education through their work within religious communities;
◆ worked with and challenged the assumptions of colleagues who perceive opposition to SRE from religious communities.

In 1992, the Sex Education Forum published a report (Thomson and Scott 1992) identifying religion and ethnicity as a significant factor in delivering effective sex education. In response we developed a resource *Religion, Ethnicity and Sex Education: Exploring the issues* (Thomson 1993). A complementary resource *Sex Education, Values and Morality* (Lenderyou and Porter 1994) was published by the Health Education Authority. Both resources aimed to support schools in responding to the challenge of developing SRE in a multi-faith and multi-cultural society. At the same time, many local and national colleagues from faith-based organisations, health promotion, education and voluntary agencies have worked with religious and faith communities on personal and social development and SRE. This resource aims to build upon the learning from this work.

The government also recognises the need to work with a multi-cultural perspective, and this is reflected in the strategies of the relevant departments. Through the *Sex and Relationship Education Guidance* (DfEE 0116/2000), the Department for Education and Skills is committed to ensuring that faith and culture are addressed as part of SRE. The Department of Health also believes that faith communities need to be involved in efforts to reduce teenage pregnancy and support young parents, and has established a Multi-Faith Forum. For further information about the Department of Health's Teenage Pregnancy Strategy or the Multi-Faith Forum visit the website www.teenagepregnancyunit.gov.uk

The SRE, Faith and Values Project

The SRE, Faith and Values Project was funded by the Teenage Pregnancy Unit to support the implementation of the new SRE Guidance from the Department for Education and Employment (0116/2000). It was carried out in a number of stages:

◆ A literature review.
◆ A national mapping exercise.
◆ A working seminar for members of the Sex Education Forum.

◆ Two national consultation days for professionals involved in delivering sex and relationships education in different settings.
◆ Consultations with children and young people from a range of different faiths.
◆ A meeting in Bradford where representatives from different religious and faith perspectives explored the issues.
◆ A two-day residential workshop with 18 people representing different faith perspectives. Participants took part in a follow up event to consult on the draft resource.

Based on the findings, we identified topics with which practitioners have been struggling in the planning and delivery of SRE. They include the moral and ethical issues underpinning an acceptable code of conduct across faiths. During the residential workshop, participants explored the issues and offered expert advice, ideas and strategies on how to resolve some of the perceived and real difficulties.

About the resource

Faith, Values and Sex and Relationships Education draws on the findings of the SRE Faith and Values Project. It focuses on strategies which schools, and others working with children and young people, can use to develop an inclusive approach to SRE. Its aims are:

◆ to support the development of SRE policy and preparation for classroom practice;
◆ to support schools in developing a framework for the provision of relevant and inclusive SRE that fulfils the entitlement of all children and young people, whatever their faith or cultural background;
◆ to provide practical ideas and strategies for schools to develop a positive consultation process with parents/carers and members of the wider community;
◆ to reduce the fear of creating conflict and causing offence, and to increase support for developing effective SRE.

Who is the resource for?

It has been designed to help teachers and other professionals whose aim is to support schools in developing and delivering sex and relationships education.

How to use the resource

The resource is divided into four main sections plus appendices:

Section 1: Putting SRE, values and the law into context explores the values underpinning the resource, looks at the legal background to SRE and sets the subject within a national policy context.

Section 2: Inclusive SRE: What needs to be in place looks at some of the issues involved in developing a policy framework and gives guidance on effective consultation. Key principles for delivering high quality SRE in the classroom are also considered, along with the importance of community-based SRE.

Section 3: Working with faith perspectives and particular topic areas gives an overview of the key values underpinning the major faiths, together with each faith's perspective on nine topics (e.g. abortion, divorce and homosexuality). It also gives guidance on addressing each topic in the classroom.

Section 4: Reviewing and developing SRE policy and practice: an agenda for action outlines a step-by-step process to develop or review SRE policy and practice. An audit tool is provided based on the criteria for the SRE theme within the National Healthy School Standard.

Appendix A: Different views on why children and young people need SRE – A list highlighting how people have many different perspectives about why children need SRE.

Appendix B: Core values and working definitions – These two lists, of core values and working definitions, are intended as a starting point to agreeing common ground during the consultation process.

Appendix C: Useful organisations gives details of who they are and what they do.

Appendix D: References – lists (in alphabetical order of authors' names) resources and other literature mentioned in this pack.

Section 1: Putting SRE, values and the law into context

1: Finding common ground

This chapter considers common myths about sex and relationships education and faith, and gives guidance for enabling people with different perspectives to communicate more effectively.

Principles underlying this resource

There are three fundamental principles underlying this resource.

◆ Children and young people have an entitlement to sex and relationships education that is relevant to them, supports them in learning about different faiths and cultures, and is underpinned by values promoting equality and respect. A range of religious and faith perspectives need to be addressed in schools and community settings, and children and young people need opportunities to understand the law and health issues in relation to sex, sexuality and sexual health. So for example, even if religious doctrine forbids sex before marriage or the use of contraception, young people need to know and understand the legal and health implications as well as different religious perspectives.

◆ Valuing diversity and anti-discriminatory practice must be an integral part of the school's ethos, reflected in all areas of the curriculum. In SRE this involves professionals taking responsibility for consulting and involving faith communities in the development of policy and practice.

◆ We need to create a safe framework in which parents and carers from faith communities, and members of the wider community, understand more about SRE, are able to discuss their views and beliefs, and to feel involved with the process of developing SRE.

Overcoming common myths about SRE, faith and values

During the SRE Faith and Values Project some persistent themes emerged, each of which is discussed in more detail below:

◆ Misunderstanding about SRE from parents and carers is common.
◆ Misunderstanding about faith perspectives on sex and sexuality is common.
◆ Misunderstanding and assumptions about faith communities' opposition to SRE are common.
◆ Misunderstanding is destructive as it impedes the development of effective SRE.

Misunderstanding about SRE

Sex and relationships education is often assumed to be a secular activity that colludes with popular culture and promotes sexual permissiveness. During the development of this pack, we were told repeatedly about the enduring belief held by some members of religious groups that SRE is delivered without a moral or values framework. Some also believe that people who deliver SRE are not concerned about when or why young people choose to have sex (Blake and Frances 2001). However, an international review of evidence (Health Development Agency 2001) shows that young people who receive SRE which meets certain criteria (see page 32) delay sexual activity and take responsibility for contraception.

The misunderstandings may be based on the premise that sex education simply means education on how to have sex. SRE is therefore seen as a secular activity and so is perceived to collude with 'immorality and popular culture'.

Colleagues involved in the project emphasised that many of the values underpinning faiths are evident within a secular perspective; so for example people without a faith tradition will also value the concepts of 'family', respect, trust and commitment.

People have many different perspectives about why children need SRE (Halstead 1998a) and some of these are highlighted in the following list. Hence it is important for schools, children and young people, parents and carers and the wider community, to work together to develop an explicit values framework for SRE.

Different views on why children and young people need SRE

- ◆ Learning the value of family life, marriage, and stable loving relationships.
- ◆ Encouraging young people to delay sexual activity.
- ◆ Developing self respect and an empathy for others.
- ◆ Learning about contraception and the range of local and national sexual health advice, contraception and support services.
- ◆ Only having sex within marriage.
- ◆ The avoidance of unplanned pregnancy.
- ◆ Safer sex and increased condom use.
- ◆ Learning the benefits of delaying sexual activity and the benefits to be gained from such a delay.
- ◆ Learning and understanding physical development at appropriate stages.
- ◆ Understanding human sexuality, reproduction, sexual health emotions and relationships.
- ◆ Learning the importance of values and individual conscience and moral considerations.
- ◆ Develop critical thinking as part of decision making.
- ◆ Learning how to recognise and avoid exploitation and abuse.

The views above tend to fall into one or more of the following categories (adapted from Halstead 1998a):

- ◆ *The health-led approach.* This usually focuses on behaviour change for medical reasons. This includes, reducing unintended teenage pregnancy, wider condom use, preventing sexually transmitted infections including HIV, and reducing shame and stigma to improve mental health and well-being.
- ◆ *The educational entitlement approach.* This is concerned with developing personal and social skills as well as beliefs, morality and values frameworks, enabling young people to formulate and live by their codes of conduct based on respect for self and others. The approach supports equality and autonomy, personal and civic responsibilities as well as understanding the law. The changing views and needs of children and young people are integral to this approach, which could be considered to represent a secular perspective.
- ◆ *The socio-economic approach.* This examines the relationships between public spending, social welfare, unplanned parenthood, poverty, unemployment and low educational attainment. It seeks to ensure that educational entitlement will provide equity, in terms of life chances and appropriate skills, for children and young people and ultimately reduce dependency on the state.
- ◆ *Religious aims for sex education* vary according to the faith and even the denomination or movement within that faith. Within SRE, they give priority to accepted codes of conduct, laws and teachings that tend to focus upon the sanctity of marriage and the procreation of children.

A common theme within *all* these approaches is that children and young people require moral guidance, knowledge, skills and positive beliefs to develop a sense of identity, self-esteem and confidence to move effectively through puberty and adolescence into adulthood.

The Sex Education Forum members have worked together and agreed the following aims for SRE.

SRE should support children and young people in managing adolescence and by preparing them for an adult life in which they can:

◆ Be aware of and enjoy their sexuality.
◆ Develop positive values and a moral framework that will guide their decisions, judgements and behaviour.
◆ Have the confidence and self-esteem to value themselves and others.
◆ Behave responsibly within sexual and personal relationships.
◆ Communicate effectively.
◆ Have sufficient information and skills to protect themselves and their partner from unintended conceptions and sexually transmitted infections including HIV.
◆ Neither exploit or be exploited.
◆ Access confidential advice and support

(SEF 1999)

Misunderstanding about faith perspectives on sex and sexuality

Religious and faith perspectives on sex and sexuality are often perceived as restrictive and as focusing on what individuals cannot or should not do. Throughout the development of this pack, the need to challenge this perception became clear along with the importance of recognising that there are positive values underpinning strict religious rules.

Religious doctrines can be viewed as a means to a spiritual goal, rather than merely a restriction on what is and is not acceptable. Moral codes of conduct are derived from religious teachings. On a spiritual level, following these moral codes can provide members of a religion with rules to live by, and consequently, can result in a profound sense of liberation. This is often unrecognised within SRE.

Some young people may experience SRE as an attempt to save them from their faith or culture (Ray 2000). This is not helpful. SRE should provide the opportunity for exploration and discussion about different perspectives to take place, so enabling young people to develop empathy and respect for diversity.

Misunderstanding and assumptions about faith communities' opposition to SRE

The perceived opposition of faith communities to SRE means that professionals are hesitant about consulting parents and others in the development of SRE. This perpetuates the misunderstandings about SRE as a secular activity and encourages suspicion.

Colleagues involved in this work suggest that if faith communities trusted that their perspectives would have a place in SRE teaching, it could help to allay some fears about the unchecked influence of popular culture and build confidence in school-based SRE. This has been confirmed by the Muslim Educational Trust in their booklet on SRE (Sarwar 1996). This states that in the planning and delivery of SRE, *'Muslims would like to be reassured that the principles of Islam are given due consideration...'* (page 7).

Halstead (1998a) also points out that ensuring the range of different views is offered within SRE is in line with good multi-cultural education and will build confidence in SRE.

Misunderstanding is destructive and disagreement is not failure

When working with diversity, consensus should not be an expected outcome of consultation. People cannot always agree. Enduring misunderstandings and differences of opinion need to be openly and respectfully placed on the agenda and clarified as part of the process whenever SRE is being discussed. Above all, it is important to remember that misunderstanding is destructive and disagreement is not failure.

By keeping the expressed needs of children and young people central to the development of SRE, it is possible to find a way forward. The experience of colleagues (Robin and others 1998) shows that parents, carers and faith leaders can develop a greater confidence in school-based SRE if we work to examine assumptions and beliefs and ensure effective communication that reduces misunderstanding. We also need to develop an explicit values framework for SRE and include a range of faith and secular perspectives in classroom practice.

2: Values within sex and relationships education

This chapter identifies different sorts of values and beliefs that underpin various approaches to sex and relationships education, and looks at the values underlying the National Curriculum.

Prescriptive and enabling values

Values can be described as either enabling or prescriptive (Lenderyou and Porter 1994). But the reality is perhaps less clear-cut. People with a faith will often interpret teachings and values based on their understanding, experience or context, and in so doing they may develop a code which draws on both types of values.

Prescriptive values

Codes of conduct are prescribed and individuals are expected and supported to live by them. The beliefs underpinning these may be seen as prescriptive, such as 'homosexuality is unacceptable' or 'sex before marriage is wrong.' These codes give guidance on how to function on spiritual, social, intellectual, cultural, emotional and physical levels. They free people to live by rules to which they may be profoundly committed, rather than having to constantly question their motives and frames of reference.

Enabling values

Enabling values tend to be more individualistic and offer a framework for developing a variety of moral codes. An example of this might be: 'sex is better when it takes place within a committed relationship based on trust, honesty and mutual respect', which reflects the educational entitlement approach to SRE described on page 7.

Enabling values tend to be the hallmark of education within our multi-cultural, multi-faith society. Effective SRE reflects this. Young people are encouraged to explore their own beliefs and values and consider how their own moral code of conduct will inform their future sexual behaviour. Enabling values underpin the explicit statement of values included in the National Curriculum (QCA/DfEE 1999).

Values in the National Curriculum

The National Curriculum is underpinned by a stated belief in education as a route to spiritual, social, cultural, physical and moral development, and hence the well-being of the individual. It has two broad aims that provide an essential context within which schools develop their own curriculum:

> **Aim 1: The school curriculum should aim to provide opportunities for all children and young people to learn and achieve.**

> **Aim 2: The school curriculum should aim to promote children and young people's spiritual, moral, social and cultural development and prepare all young people for the opportunities and responsibilities of life.**

These two aims enable children and young people to develop the knowledge and understanding of their own and different beliefs in an equal opportunities framework. They will be able to understand their rights and responsibilities; develop enduring values, and respect for their communities. It promotes their self-esteem and emotional well-being and helps them to form and maintain satisfying relationships. Personal, Social and Health Education (PSHE) and Citizenship – of which SRE is a key part – are central to achieving these aims (see pages 17–18).

Ensuring equal opportunities and equal treatment in SRE

The right of individuals to fair and equitable treatment in health and education is enshrined in an equal opportunities philosophy. Equal opportunities issues are never simple, but may pose a particular challenge in SRE (Thomson 1993). For example, professionals involved in the consultation reflected:

> **'How can we meet the needs of those who are gay, lesbian or bisexual while respecting religious and cultural beliefs?'**

> **'We think that all young people need information about abortion and contraception, yet some schools will not teach about it because of their religious ethos.'**

So we can see here how tensions between religious and cultural practices and the concept of equal opportunities can serve to undermine the confidence of teachers and others in delivering SRE. One of the key questions asked during the development of this pack was, 'How do we balance the needs and wants of parents, carers and children and young people?' It is important to acknowledge that we may not be able to meet the needs of both. Focusing on the needs of the pupil, and adopting an anti-discriminatory approach to the consultation process with parents/carers and the community, will go some way to resolving potential conflicts.

Case study: Quakers give guidance to faith members on being inclusive

The national guidance below has been developed by Quakers to ensure that group work at Quaker gatherings is inclusive.

When developing group work at Quaker events, we try to create and maintain an environment where everyone can gain something. People taking part in activities will have different experiences, talents, and life journeys. Our aim is to create a time where we can share and learn together. The diversity within the group provides great opportunities and, when encouraged, all participants can contribute in their own way.

We hope that the following questions will help you to make your work as inclusive as possible:

Do you make assumptions that everyone understands 'Quaker Speak', initials and long words?
It is helpful to explain things in simple plain English, not assuming understanding of Quaker language.

Have you made assumptions that all young Quakers are 'white, middle class, well-educated, heterosexual, preferably in stable marriages with children who behave in socially accepted ways'? (Quaker Faith & Practice)

Are you or can you imagine being different from that stereotype – how would you feel if involved in the exercise or programme that you have designed?

Do you encourage people to think more about their ideas and opinions through thoughtful questioning?
People may make statements or repeat other people's ideas without realising the implications. Prompt involvement with comments such as 'Can you tell us more about that?' or 'Can you give us an example of that?', can help participants think more deeply about a statement.

How can you include participants whose opinions challenge your own values and principles, or whose opinions appear to set them apart from the group?
As Quakers, we believe that our faith is developed and understood from our individual experience. When participants trust and share their ideas and beliefs, differences may be highlighted and conflicts can occur. As facilitator, you are providing a safe learning environment not providing a 'correct answer'. It is not necessary to arrive at consensus or agreement. If possible, give value to the contributor, even if the opinion is contrary to yours or the group's accepted beliefs and values. It can be helpful to acknowledge the differences, and encourage people to continue the discussion at another time.

Does your activity/programme use a variety of methods and skills?
Some people prefer writing and discussions, others drawing and making things. Try to be creative in your planning.

When giving instructions for an activity, are you clear and concise, checking out that participants have understood?
Give examples of what you mean when explaining activities, and allow opportunities for people to ask clarifying questions.

Have you been clear where and how information will be shared?
People may trust a partner with spoken or written information in a pair activity they would not wish to

share with the wider group. Be clear about how information will be shared, who will provide feedback and to whom when explaining the exercise.

Do you include a variety of ways of recording information and responses?
If it is important to record responses, use a taped comment or photos or symbols that prompt ideas. If you need to write up feedback, ask volunteers to write, and read out what is written so that people who can't read English can still know what is written.

Do you give information as a series of points rather than in long paragraphs?
Using bullet points written in different, strong colours help people with dyslexia to read more easily. When giving typewritten sheets, space out paragraphs, and use clear simple fonts with a point size 12, and leave ragged edges at the right hand side.

Can you use colour creatively to help understanding and make the event fun learning?
Different coloured paper for each handout, or using a logo to identify a particular set of items can help recognition.

Does the programme/exercise provide a balance of active and quieter activities?
Concentration and interest spans vary and it is helpful to have a few activities that can develop more if there is interest and enthusiasm.

Can you think of more ways of ensuring an environment where people feel included, respected and safe?

Please add your ideas to ours and let us know.

Taken from *Only Quaker Pack*, Chambers and others. E-mail ql@quaker.org.uk.

How specific values underpin different faiths and cultures

Faiths hold a set of beliefs that people ascribe to. As a result, they adopt certain practices which provide a framework for their behaviour.

Culture is alive and evolving and is concerned with how we behave together when part of a group with a recognised identity. It may relate to what is considered acceptable in terms of, for example, marriage and other customs, dress, food and other areas. It is something that we own, both subconsciously and consciously, because we are aware of the cultural norms of our chosen community. We recognise certain ways of thinking, behaving and talking to be acceptable. Cultures change and evolve. Religious teachings are interpreted within this changing culture although the core philosophy remains broadly the same.

Culture relies on the majority of a group agreeing on how to behave with each other through work, education, religion, literature, art, socially and so on. Set codes of conduct develop, based on values systems that are understood by those who wish to be part of the culture. The group is also aware of historical influences on its culture. It is important however to recognise the interconnections between religious and cultural identity. Often culture and religion become confused and are considered inter-changeable. Cultural practices – such as girls keeping their hair long, men taking responsibility, women obeying their husbands, or female genital mutilation – are sometimes inaccurately assumed to be based upon religious doctrine.

Within a multi-cultural society, dominant cultural norms can devalue difference by perceiving it as a threat, by 'ironing out' the problem of difference, or by ignoring its existence. Minority cultures may guard against assimilation and discrimination by creating very public and well-defined parameters.

Culture by its very definition is ever changing. Children and young people are part of this process of change. They belong to a variety of cultural and sub-cultural groups and SRE should take account of this. It should provide opportunities for them to look at the connections between religion, culture (including peer and local norms) and ethnicity and how they fit together, as a means of exploring their own identity.

It is important too, to remember that there is diversity of beliefs within faiths and a diversity of faiths within ethnicities. For instance, it may seem reasonable to assume that the majority of Hindus, Muslims and Sikhs are South or South East Asian or Middle Eastern, or the majority of Christians and Jews are white-European in origin. However, while ethnicity is broadly visible, a person's faith is not necessarily visible unless identifiable by symbols such as dress or different naming systems.

Conversely, in writing about faith, whole ethnic communities can seem to disappear from view because faith groups can be so multi-ethnic in nature. For instance, people of African, African-Caribbean, Chinese or Vietnamese origin – who might be Christian, Buddhist or Muslim – may be rendered invisible if we lose awareness of the geographical and historical impact of the major religions and their influence on multi-ethnic communities in Britain today.

The Sex Education Forum is currently running a project focusing on the needs of black and minority ethnic children and young people, and the resource will accompany and complement this pack.

The seven dimensions of a religion Adapted from *The World's Religions* (Smart 1989)

Below, the author, Ninian Smart, identifies the seven different dimensions of religion. These dimensions help to explain the holistic and all encompassing nature of religion and the central role that religion can play in some children and young people's lives. The approach also highlights often ignored aspects of religious identity as well as demonstrating how spiritual fulfilment within religion can provide an emotional dimension for which there is no counterpart within secular cultures. It may also help to provide an arena where 'different but equal' can be recognised.

1. The practical and ritual dimensions
> Every tradition has some practices to which it adheres, e.g. worship, preaching, prayers, meditation, yoga, sacrifice etc. There are also formal and explicit ceremonies and rites of religion.

2. The experiential and emotional dimension

In understanding a religion's tradition, it is important to try to enter into the feelings which it generates – to feel 'the sacred awe, the calm peace, the rousing inner dynamism, the perception of a brilliant emptiness within, the outpouring of love, the sensation of hope…' Mystical experiences lie at the heart of all the major religions.

3. The narrative or mythic dimension

It is typical of faiths to hand down vital stories. Stories of creation predate history, as do myths which indicate how death and suffering came into the world. Some stories are about historical events, for instance the life of the Prophet Mohammed, the execution of Jesus, or the enlightenment of the Buddha. They are often integrated with the ritual dimension, e.g. Mass or communion commemorating the Last Supper, Passover ceremonies and the Exodus.

4. The doctrinal and philosophical dimensions

Underpinning the narrative dimension is the doctrinal dimension. This allows for the analysis of the nature of the Divine, e.g. the Holy Trinity or exploration of the doctrine of the Buddha. This provides an essential intellectual component to religion.

5. The ethical and legal dimension

Both narrative and doctrine affect the values of a tradition by laying out a world view and addressing the question of ultimate liberation or salvation. The religious laws incorporated into a tradition are the ethical dimension. For example in Buddhism there are the five precepts, in Christianity the ten commandments. Laws can shape society both as a religious and political society, as well as the moral life of the individual. Ethics can be controlled by myth and doctrine, e.g. God is love, flowing from the Trinity, Christ is the suffering servant of the human race and all creation.

6. The social and institutional dimension

To understand a faith we need to see how it works among the people. Every religious movement is embodied in a group of people, and that is often formally organised, e.g. the Sangha, the Church etc. This is the sociology of religion. There are many different types of relationships between organised religions and society at large: a faith may be the official religion, just one denomination, or cut off from society like a cult or sect. There are many models within the organisation of one religion from democratic governance to hierarchical and monarchical systems.

7. The material dimension

The social and institutional dimension of religion almost inevitably becomes incarnate in material forms such as buildings, works of art and artefacts, natural features such as sacred rivers (the Ganges), mountains (Mount Fuji) etc, and sacred landmarks combined with human creations such as the holy city of Jerusalem, sacred shrines of Benares or the temple at Bodh Gaya. Material expressions of religion are important for believers in their approach to the divine.

3: The legal and policy context for SRE

The **1996 Education Act** consolidated all relevant previous legislation. In summary:

◆ The biological elements of sex and relationships education in the **National Curriculum Science Order** are mandatory for all pupils of primary and secondary age across all key stages.

◆ All schools must provide an up-to-date policy that describes the content and organisation of SRE provided outside the National Curriculum Science Order. It is the school governors' responsibility to ensure that the policy is developed and made available to parents for inspection.

◆ Primary schools should have a policy statement describing the SRE provided, or giving a statement of the decision not to provide SRE other than what is provided within the National Curriculum Science Order.

◆ Secondary schools are required to provide an SRE programme that includes (as a minimum) information about sexually transmitted infections and HIV/AIDS.

In practice most schools aim to provide a broad and balanced SRE curriculum that includes the three elements of skills, information and values.

The national context

The Teenage Pregnancy Strategy

The Teenage Pregnancy Strategy (Social Exclusion Unit 1999) was launched by Tony Blair in June 1999. The strategy sets out a comprehensive action plan to reduce the rate of teenage pregnancies by 50 per cent by 2010 with an interim target of 15 per cent by 2004. It also aims to reduce the long-term social exclusion of young parents through a series of measures. Among a whole raft of action points, a key element of the strategy is to improve sex and relationships education to combat ignorance and a culture of silence and embarrassment surrounding sex and relationships.

The National Healthy School Standard

The NHSS is a national programme with a regional and local network. Every LEA has developed a local programme in partnership with health. The programme offers training, support and an accreditation process for schools. There is a national target for all schools to be involved in a nationally accredited local healthy school programme by 2002. A healthy school provides an environment in which children and young people can do 'their best'.

The NHSS stresses the importance of diversity and equality issues, explicitly referring to religious diversity. The national programme provides a robust and flexible framework within which local areas and schools can respond to the specific needs of their children and young people.

Healthy schools work with children and young people, parents, carers and staff, as well as other members of the school community, to develop activities that will support both the raising of education standards and improvements in health. This is done within both the formal curriculum and is demonstrated within the general ethos and climate of the school. SRE is one of the key themes alongside drug education, safety, physical activity and emotional health and well-being.

A whole school approach

The NHSS identifies the importance of a whole school approach to children and young people's emotional and social development. Children and young people learn about sex and relationships from all sorts of people and places, not just in formal SRE classes. They learn by observing how adults behave with each other and with them, and by seeing what is considered acceptable behaviour.

The school ethos needs to support and reflect the positive messages about sex and relationships that are offered within SRE. Children and young people need to see adults modelling positive relationships and respect for diversity. With specific reference to this pack, it is important to acknowledge the range of religious festivals and holidays, and ensure that the school promotes understanding and respect for the different faiths and cultures within the school community.

Further information can be found in the National Healthy School Standard documents *Guidance* and *Getting Started* (NHSS 1999a, b). There is also a supporting document for local programmes focusing specifically on SRE (NHSS 2001).

PSHE and Citizenship in schools

In 1999, the Government published the first ever Personal, Social, Health Education (PSHE) and Citizenship framework (QCA/DfEE 1999). PSHE is non-statutory at Key Stages 1-4. At Key Stages 3 and 4 there is a statutory requirement for Citizenship from 2002. This unified framework has four strands and provides a planning tool to assist schools in meeting the central aims of the National Curriculum through a holistic approach to PSHE and Citizenship.

The four strands are:

◆ develop confidence and make the most of their abilities;
◆ prepare to play an active role as citizens;

◆ develop a healthy, safer lifestyle;

◆ develop good relationships and respect differences between people.

PSHE and Citizenship provide a framework for exploring religion, faith, sex, sexuality and relationships, and SRE is an integral part of its remit. Through PSHE and Citizenship, children and young people develop confidence and skills, including the ability to explore their values and attitudes with peers and adults. It also enables them to make decisions based on sound information; and to develop critical thinking and moral reasoning.

SRE begins in the early years. The early learning goals lay the foundation for emotional and social development. Children learn about sex and relationships from an early age, often informally from friends and peers, through the media and by watching the adults around them.

OfSTED (2002) suggests that, at the end of Key Stage 1, within SRE, children should be able to recognise similarities and differences between themselves and others, treat others with sensitivity and understand how their feelings and actions impact on other people. By the end of Key Stage 2, children should be able to see things from different perspectives and have thought about the diversity of values and customs in the school and the community.

This will then be built upon in the secondary years where OfSTED recommend that pupils should have begun to grasp the complexity of topical, moral, social and cultural issues and be able to form a view of their own. They should also have developed empathy with core values underpinning family life in all its variety of forms. By the end of Key Stage 4, OfSTED recommends that pupils will have thought about how personal, family and social values influence behaviour and the arguments about moral issues such as abortion, contraception and IVF treatment.

The SRE Guidance (2000) is supported in legislation by the **Learning and Skills Act (2000)** which requires that pupils learn about the nature of marriage and its importance for family life, and are protected from teaching and materials which are inappropriate for the age and the religious and cultural background of the pupils concerned.

Citizenship education becomes statutory at Key Stages 3 and 4 and provides exciting opportunities for exploring religion, faith, sex, sexuality and relationships. Within Citizenship, children and young people learn about the diversity of national, regional, religious and ethnic identities within the UK and the need for mutual respect and understanding. It also requires that children and young people develop skills of enquiry and communication and are provided with opportunities to research topical political, spiritual, moral, social or cultural issues.

Section 2: Inclusive SRE: What needs to be in place

4: Developing SRE policy

Why a policy is needed

The Sex and Relationship Education Guidance from the DfEE states:

> **'SRE should contribute to promoting the spiritual, moral, cultural, mental and physical development of pupils at school and of society and preparing pupils for the opportunities, responsibilities and experiences of adult life.'**

It recommends that schools have an overall PSHE policy within which SRE will be a discrete part. It emphasises that for many children and young people, schools will be the main source of information and education about sex and relationships. The importance of developing policies that are both 'culturally appropriate and inclusive of all children' is also stressed:

> **'Primary and secondary schools should consult parents and pupils, both on what is included and how it should be delivered. For example, for some children it is not culturally appropriate to address particular issues in a mixed group. Consulting pupils and their families will help establish what is appropriate and acceptable for them.'**

It emphasises that both pupils and parents/carers may need reassurance that the personal beliefs and attitudes of teachers will not influence the teaching of SRE. Teachers and all those contributing to SRE are expected to work within an agreed values framework, which must be in line with current legislation, using a planned curriculum, methodology and resources as described in the school's policy.

A model policy framework can be found on the Sex Education Forum website www.ncb.org.uk/sexed.htm

A moral and values framework for SRE

The policy includes a moral and values framework. The revised National Curriculum (QCA/DfEE 1999) has an explicit statement of values which promotes respect for self, others, society and the environment. The core values of justice, responsibility, care, love, commitment, marriage, protection and preservation are also highlighted. Assumptions and views about SRE, shared by institutions, teachers, children and young people, and parents and carers, need to be explored and an explicit values framework developed.

Teachers and others working with young people may worry that exploring issues such as abortion, sex outside marriage, homosexuality, contraception and safer sex for example, will be unacceptable to some parents and carers from traditional faith communities. They may therefore prepare to defend themselves against a fear of attack, rather than creating opportunities for dialogue. Such a dialogue may initially prove uncomfortable but if done well, results in SRE being developed in which faith and secular perspectives are integrated.

Another concern is which values should be promoted within SRE. The statement of values in the National Curriculum Handbooks and the school's mission statement provide a good starting point from which to consult with parents, carers and the community in order to develop an agreed values framework for SRE. See Appendix B for a list of core values.

Schools with a religious character

All schools will have a particular ethos and set of values that SRE should build upon and support. Schools with a religious character will have an ethos and values that reflects their particular beliefs, and the values promoted in SRE should reflect this. However it is important that all schools enable children and young people to explore and understand that people have different values and beliefs, and that they know and understand their legal rights.

Specific issues

The policy will also need to include a section on specific issues, such as whether single gender groups will be used, when and how this will be organised, and how resources will be chosen and used.

Single gender groups

There will be occasions when it is helpful to work in single gender groups for some aspects of SRE. For some, it may not be culturally acceptable to talk about sex and relationships in mixed gender groups (DfEE 2000). This can considerably ease parents', carers' and others' concerns about SRE, and help to ensure that children and young people receive entitlement to SRE.

Single gender groups can also help boys and girls to feel safer and less embarrassed about airing issues and discussing relationships.

> **'I wouldn't want to talk about certain things in front of the boys.'**
> *Young Muslim woman, aged 15*

Choosing and using resources

The checklist below provides useful pointers on selecting and using resources in SRE.

Checklist for selecting a resource for health/sex education

✓ Is it consistent with the school ethos, mission statement, equal opportunities statement and the values framework for SRE?

✓ Is it appropriate to the needs of your young people in terms of language, images, attitude, maturity and understanding and the knowledge required?

✓ Does it avoid racism, sexism, gender and homophobic stereotyping? Does it exclude any young people on the basis of home circumstance, gender, race, literacy, culture, disability, faith, and religion?

✓ Does it include positive images of a range of young people?

✓ Can it be used as trigger material for discussions of difference or exclusiveness?

✓ Can the resource be adapted for use with all of your young people?

✓ Is it factually correct and up-to-date?

✓ Will it contribute to a broad and balanced PSHE and Citizenship curriculum?

✓ Does it encourage active and participatory learning methods?

✓ If you have used this resource before what formal or informal feedback did you receive from children and young people about it?

Outside visitors

> **'I felt more comfortable talking to Mrs. Green because she made it really interesting and let you know where to go if you wanted personal advice.'**
> *Young Muslim woman, aged 16*

The benefits of using visitors within school PSHE and Citizenship lessons are well understood and schools may wish to use outside visitors for some aspects of SRE. OfSTED (2002) reported that outside visitors make a significant contribution to SRE. Outside visitors need to agree to work within the school's values framework. It is not good practice to allow visitors who try to frighten children and young people, or provide factually incorrect information. (This often happens in relation to termination of pregnancy and is not helpful for the young people involved.)

Children and young people will get most out of an outside visitor if they have prepared well and there is adequate follow up time. Their questions could be sent to the visitor in advance so they can ensure that the lesson is relevant and the children and young people are given responsibility for their learning.

Loco parentis (in the position of parent) remains with the teacher when an outside visitor is leading a class and it is important that the teacher and visitor have agreed roles and responsibilities so that they do not undermine each other.

The Jewish AIDS Trust (JAT) provide outside visitors to (mainly Jewish) schools. The majority of the work takes place in London, particularly in North London where there is the most significant Jewish community. The target audience is Jewish youth, most of whom are between ages 12 and 18. They also lead workshops for youth workers and for adult groups who want to learn more about HIV and AIDS. Education sessions include:

◆ the 'science' of HIV – how it is transmitted, how to protect yourself from contracting HIV;
◆ considering which bodily fluids are infectious;
◆ considering which activities are "high risk" (injecting drugs, unsafe sex, etc.);
◆ Jewish perspectives on HIV – why it is important to take care of the ill in our community, what does Judaism say about sex, drugs, etc;
◆ scenarios – to examine the stigmas attached to HIV, to think about how best to interact with those living with HIV;
◆ condom demonstrations – how to properly apply a condom and what are other methods of contraception (many do not protect against STIs);
◆ decision making skills – how to say no, how to decide if you are ready for the consequences of being sexually active;
◆ challenging homophobia – how are we obligated to treat gays and lesbians in the Jewish community.

For further information contact the Jewish AIDS Trust www.jat-uk.org

5: Effective consultation

Effective consultation, built on the principle of valuing diversity (see working definitions, Apendix A), lies at the heart of high quality sex and relationships education. 'Diversity' is a concept that recognises the benefits to be gained from difference. Valuing diversity is about seeking to include and involve groups and individuals from many sections of society rather than the more powerful few. The strengths present in diversity can then be utilised proactively and positively for the benefit of all.

This chapter offers some pointers on carrying out the consultation process and gives positive examples of consultations with parents, children and young people, and other groups.

The consultation process

Rationale
◆ Recognise that as professionals it is your responsibility to include different people.
◆ Professional attitudes of inclusion must take precedence over personal feelings in a situation of conflict.
◆ Understand that consensus is not necessary and that disagreement is not failure.
◆ Be clear about the school's values framework, the law, guidance and faith perspectives.
◆ Be clear about the school's aims for SRE, entitlement of young people and the health and education benefits of SRE.

Preparation
◆ Recognise that conflict often arises from people misunderstanding each other, not disagreeing with each other.
◆ Understand the situation as one where two 'sides' may be miscommunicating based on assumptions of the other's viewpoints rather than through an understanding and constructive dialogue.
◆ Recognise and believe in the positive intentions of the majority of people involved in the consultation.
◆ Recognise that communication across cultural boundaries requires skilful handling.
◆ Avoid viewing religious teachings as either the 'problem' or the 'answer'.
◆ Be aware of and responsible for your power base in relation to your professional position.

Process
◆ Do not expect reciprocated respect until trust is established.
◆ Be prepared to use skills of professional empathy in situations of conflict.

◆ Be prepared to listen to contradictory and hostile opinions and attitudes without feeling personally challenged.
◆ Be prepared with a coherent explanation of your values framework and how these relate to the wider context of the school mission and ethos.
◆ Recognise that discussion of core values can support positive dialogue and be pro-active in exploring values and their meaning.
◆ Feel confident enough to explain that faith perspectives will be included as part of the continuum of perspectives which also contains the teaching of equality, freedom from discrimination and individual rights.

Avoiding hostility

In any consultation process, it is crucial that people feel that they are being heard and understood. Otherwise tensions can quickly rise leading to feelings of anger and frustration as the example below illustrates.

What can happen

Person A makes a point.

Person B makes assumptions and expresses those assumptions in response to that point without checking out the meaning with person A. Person B has misunderstood the point.

Person A begins to feel annoyed and defensive. Emotional reaction of justification takes over from the intellectual response of clarifying the meaning of their original point.

The interaction then escalates based on misunderstanding – as the assumption rather than the true meaning of the point is being debated and doubly clouded by irrational feelings of for example anger or fear.

How the facilitator can help

Person A: I think that it is really important that boys and girls start to learn about sex and relationships when they are in primary school.

Person B: So you don't think it matters that it might encourage them to have sex?

Facilitator: Can you say a bit more about why you think it might encourage them to have sex?

The role of the facilitator can be crucial in ensuring that a consultation process works and they will play a key role in ensuring that misunderstanding is clarified. Facilitators need to demonstrate that they hear and value the right of others to hold different perspectives and should also give equal prominence to these diverse views while highlighting common ground.

Case study: Bradford: The consultation process in an inter-faith setting

Bradford LEA and Interfaith Education Centre worked with the Sex Education Forum to hold a meeting that explored the role and purpose of sex and relationships education. Participants were invited through the local Standing Advisory Committee on Religious Education.

The meeting took place at the Interfaith Education Centre, Bradford, and over 20 participants from the major faiths of the city were present including Muslim, Hindu, Sikh, Bahai and Christian. The aim of the project was highlighted and information was given about how SRE fits into PSHE as well as the wider perspectives of Citizenship, NHSS, the SRE Guidance and the importance of RE. Generally participants confirmed the need for high quality SRE and emphasised the importance of including different faith perspectives.

The group split into four smaller groups to discuss the issues and concerns that members had about any aspect of SRE. These included the following:
◆ The importance of God and religious teachings are ignored in SRE, and that parents are responsible for guiding their children.
◆ Teachers should receive training and support to teach SRE with reference to faith communities.
◆ Young people's needs should also be assessed and met appropriately.
◆ Oppression, for instance, in anti-religious attitudes, homophobia or sexism, needs to be addressed.
 Participants were then given lists of suggested topics to be covered for all the key stages, in order to discuss what could be acceptable within different faith perspectives. The debate focused on how these topics would be taught.

Issues and themes
The key issues or themes that came out of the discussion included the following:
◆ Schools need to understand the absolute commitment to God or religious teachings as a choice that benefits members of a religion.
◆ Participants will begin to trust the school-based SRE if they believe that different faith perspectives would be included.
◆ Can moral absolutists and moral relativists work together for the benefit of all our children?
◆ Some still believe that SRE is largely a secular and valueless activity and wanted an explicit values framework

There was great interest in developing an approach for SRE that could include faith perspectives. The LEA and Interfaith Education Centre have continued to develop their SRE policy and practice in response to some of the issues raised.

Positive strategies

Below are some positive strategies for consulting with different partners.

Consulting with children and young people

This can be done in a number of ways, for example, through one or more of the following:

◆ the school council;
◆ classroom surveys;
◆ SRE monitoring and assessing;
◆ information communication technology (ICT) on the website;
◆ questionnaire at a health day.

Case study: Consulting young people about their views on SRE

The Sex Education Forum and the National Children's Bureau worked with a group of young people to develop a video resource *Sex and Relationships, Myths and Education – young people's views* (2002) for use with parents/carers and governors in developing SRE policy and practice. They expressed the following desires from their SRE:

◆ Factual information, before they start puberty, before they have relationships and before they have sex.
◆ To explore and develop skills such as how to be yourself in a relationship.
◆ To think about and develop views on issues such as sexuality, contraception, sex before marriage and teenage pregnancy.
◆ To think about what it means to be in a relationship, when the right time to have sex is, and other real life situations which they described as 'dilemmas'.

Consulting with governors

Governors are responsible for ensuring that the school has an SRE policy. Some governors will not understand the importance of SRE or may be suspicious of its content. It is important to secure their commitment and involvement. One strategy might be to ask representatives from the school council to talk about why an SRE policy is important and what they think is needed. Alternatively, a survey of children and young people's views on SRE could be circulated and comments invited.

Consulting with parents and carers

National surveys have shown that parents/carers are generally supportive of SRE (NFER/HEA 1994). Consultation with parents/carers about the content and organisation of SRE is likely to build their confidence and avoid some of the common misunderstandings (Scott 1996). Consultation can take place through specific meetings on SRE or through more general PSHE and Citizenship meetings. Research has shown that parents/carers can be nervous about going to meetings on sex and relationships education, so it may be more effective to hold a meeting on the broader PSHE and Citizenship curriculum (Carerra and Ingham 1998).

Consideration needs to be given to:

◆ how parents/carers will be invited (for example by phone or letter);
◆ the language that is used for the invitations and whether there is any need for a translator;
◆ the timing of meetings;
◆ whether meetings should be single or mixed gender.

A very small number of parents/carers choose to withdraw their children from SRE lessons. Latest figures show that about four children will be withdrawn in every ten thousand (0.04 per cent) (OfSTED 2002).

In developing this pack we recognised that some parents/carers will withdraw their children even after effective consultation. This is not necessarily a sign that schools are doing a bad job; some parents/carers believe that it is their responsibility to educate their children about sex and relationships. In this type of situation it is important that the SRE programme is not significantly compromised to meet the needs of a tiny minority. However it may be appropriate for schools to offer parents/carers leaflets or details of organisations that can support them in talking to their child. The Department for Education and Skills also provides a leaflet for parents/carers who withdraw their children from SRE. (A leaflet for parents excluding their children from school SRE is available by phoning DfES publications – 0845 602 2260 quoting reference code DfES 0706/2001 or www.dfes.gov.uk/sreandparents.)

Two examples of an effective consultation process are provided in the case studies that follow.

Case study: Consultation with Turkish Muslim parents on SRE in girls' school

A group of Turkish Muslim parents in London were involved in a consultation on SRE for Years 7, 9 and 10 at a girls' school in a multi-racial area. During the project, the Sex Education Forum worked alongside a voluntary health-based organisation that had experience engaging with Turkish communities. Senior management at the school, along with a Turkish-speaking link worker and a Turkish-speaking member of staff, were actively involved in all the consultation sessions. A short letter was drafted in Turkish and sent to parents from the school inviting them to participate in a lunchtime meeting in order to raise any areas of concern about their daughters' education. (Three lunchtime sessions were organised as many parents worked in the evenings.) The head teacher attended each session to support the parents and facilitators.

Process

Discussions, which were facilitated in Turkish, were initially general. Gradually the facilitators led the debate towards the physical and emotional well-being of their children, and then the importance of sexual health issues for young people within the Turkish community. The parents were invited to view the resources that were being used with their children in PSHE lessons and to give feedback.

Issues

Parents clearly expected and wanted to be involved in all aspects of their daughters' education. They felt that the school was best placed to discuss sex and relationships with the girls but in consultation with them, particularly in respect of culturally appropriate behaviour. Noting that cultural taboos made it difficult for them to raise these issues with their daughters, they stressed that they wanted them to be prepared for life in England. They also praised the school's proactive approach in facilitating these sessions. The parents appreciated the head teacher attending each session, feeling that it gave the work respect and authority.

Outcomes

The process enabled the parents to speak directly with the head teacher both about the content and process of teaching SRE. It strengthened their relationship with the school and reinforced their confidence in the teachers' abilities to deliver accurate, objective information about sex and relationships. It also reassured parents that the topics being discussed in SRE could help their children to avoid abusive and exploitative situations and would reinforce their physical and emotional safety.

The perceptions of some staff were also challenged. Some had believed that no one would be interested in attending the sessions, while others had felt that any discussion would result in girls being withdrawn from SRE lessons.

Case study: Consultation with Asian women in Edinburgh

Over the past two years, the 'English as an Additional Language' Service in Edinburgh has been working with secondary schools to improve links with minority ethnic parents, and to encourage them to listen to parents' views. Schools had become concerned that parents in minority groups were withdrawing children from sexual heath education programmes and they had decided to ask parent themselves whether their materials and approaches were culturally sensitive enough.

Issues and outcomes

Several meetings took place with mainly Muslim and Sikh women. During the consultation, most of the women said they felt that sex is too explicit in our society and that young people are exposed to media bombardment of sexual images and language, which are frequently offensive to minorities. For this reason alone, a majority of the women believed that sex education should be taught in schools, so that students can learn about it properly.

Another common view was that virginity before marriage has huge cultural and religious significance for both boys and girls in Islam, as in many other religions. Premarital sexual activity is totally forbidden and could damage someone's whole life, and that of their family.

As part of SRE children and young people should become aware of a number of different cultures and religious groups, and that a number of these forbid sex outside marriage. This would make any such programme much more acceptable to many minority groups, the women said. They also felt that single sex classes would make SRE more acceptable.

A further view voiced by a significant number of the women, was that while virginity is paramount, if young people 'make a mistake' they should not feel their world must end. No one wants suicides to happen. It is therefore good that the later stages of programmes include information about sources of help and advice.

The findings are being used in staff training and the materials may be adapted into a training resource. A detailed report for schools is also available. Contact Eileen Simpson, Development Officer, by telephone 0131 556 6198, or e-mail at eileen.simpson@drummond.edin.sch.uk

Consulting with the wider community

Consultation with the wider community helps to build support for school-based SRE and ensures that there are consistent values being promoted across different settings. In planning and implementing the consultation, it is helpful to draw upon the skills and perspectives of a wide range of professionals and individuals, including ConneXions advisors, learning mentors, the school nurse, the local healthy schools coordinator and representatives from faith communities.

Case study: Northumberland Sex Education Forum (NorSEF)

NorSEF is a county-wide Sex Education Forum for those involved in the planning and delivery of SRE to young people in a variety of settings. Faith schools and church representatives have participated since the Forum was established in September 2000.

Faith representatives and others from the local community attended a consultation day at which a set of values and principles underpinning SRE were agreed and to which members of NorSEF sign up. Most faith schools in the area wanted to receive training, advice and support in delivering SRE to young people. Many were concerned about current rates of unintended teenage conceptions.

Issues and outcomes
A values group is being set up to validate resources and projects based on the agreed values and principles of NorSEF. Representatives from faith communities have been invited to join this sub-group.

NorSEF has provided a mechanism for faith groups to meet on a regular basis with others involved in the promotion and delivery of SRE and to receive support in taking forward this work. Many partnerships have evolved and health staff and youth workers work alongside teachers to deliver SRE in many settings, including faith schools. Members of NorSEF have reported that they feel less isolated in this sensitive and sometimes challenging area of work. Because the work of NorSEF is based on evidence of what works and is underpinned by a set of moral values and principles, it enables members to facilitate the delivery of SRE programmes for all young people and provides a base to negotiate with those who have concerns about providing such information to young people.

Case study: Kirklees LEA address Islamic perspectives on SRE

Kirklees Local Education Authority worked with the local council and community workers to run consultation groups and to develop a document that schools could use to address Islamic perspectives in sex and relationships education. The project was in response to local need, as many Muslim parents were not consenting to their children attending sex education classes.

Process

Seven women and eleven men from the local community were recruited to two separate discussion groups – one male and one female. Ages ranged from early twenties up to late forties, with occupations including teachers, housewives and Imams. Each participant was paid a small fee.

The groups provided an opportunity to discuss SRE provision within schools and to identify areas of concern upon which further development work would be centred. It became clear that it was not the content of the sex education classes they were objecting to, but the context in which key issues were being communicated. For instance, participants felt that the only acceptable way in which sex could be discussed was within the context of marriage. After the fifth or sixth session the two groups merged and discussed the issues openly and respectfully in a mixed group. Children and young people who had received sex education classes were also consulted to find out how useful they had found them to be. They also suggested ways in which they felt SRE could be improved.

A document was then drafted giving guidelines for schools on how to make the curriculum more relevant to Muslim children and young people. Meetings were then held with teaching staff to obtain feedback. Finally, the draft document was sent to a number of Islamic scholars for comment, approval and eventually endorsement of the document.

Issues and outcomes

It became clear that understanding local politics can help to avoid unconscious exclusion of individuals. For instance, one woman did not take part because her local mosque did not endorse the venue.

Realistic timescales are also crucial. It took far longer to receive feedback, than was anticipated. Ensuring that everyone taking part felt able to own the document was also important, enabling confidence to develop in school-based SRE.

Finally, facilitators noted that terminology sometimes caused embarrassment. Children and young people and community members found the word 'sex' embarrassing, as if use of this word implied a more permissive attitude to relationships. Emphasis on the word 'relationships' and increased understanding of the diverse issues covered in SRE allayed fears of too much emphasis on sex.

Case study: Developing SRE and sexual health work in the community

North West Health Promotion Service has worked with a range of organisations to develop SRE and sexual health work in the community. Projects have been developed in response to needs analysis and community consultation and include working with parents to review school-based SRE. Other initiatives include single gender group work and residential events.

This work has developed in partnership with a range of organisations including:

◆ Racial Equality Council
◆ Youth and Community Service
◆ Moor Park High School
◆ Gujarat Hindu Society
◆ Preston Muslim Forum
◆ Preston Sikh Cultural Association
◆ Shree Prajapati Association
◆ Lancashire Council of Mosques
◆ Local community and self help groups to develop sexual health work in schools and the community.

Three resources are available: *Rishtae aur Zimmervarian – Relationships and responsibility* (Robin, Singh and Thompson 1995) (a report and training pack) and *Mazhab and Sexuality* (Northwest Lancashire HPU) (a discussion paper).

6: Delivering SRE in the classroom

Inclusive sex and relationships education needs to be delivered in a way that engages young people and involves them in their own learning. This chapter focuses on the use of active learning methods and highlights the importance of celebrating diversity and including different perspectives across faiths and cultures.

What sort of SRE should we delivering?

SRE needs to be developed in line with the best available evidence as to what works. As already discussed, it should form part of an overall PSHE and Citizenship programme that aims to improve children and young people's self-esteem and support their emotional and social development. It should also be based upon the developmental and expressed needs of children and young people and be mindful of their previous experience (Sex Education Forum 1999).

In developing the teenage pregnancy action plan, the Social Exclusion Unit commissioned an international review of the evidence as to what works in SRE. The review concluded that the common components of effective SRE should:

◆ empower children and young people;
◆ offer a positive and open view of sex and sexuality, and support sexual self acceptance;
◆ be well linked to contraceptive services;
◆ be sustained by working within a theoretical framework;
◆ meet local needs;
◆ ensure the entitlement of all children to sex and relationships education and undertake specific work to meet the needs of vulnerable and marginalised children and young people;
◆ be provided early; before puberty, before feelings of sexual attraction and before they develop sexual relationships;
◆ reinforce value messages;
◆ focus on risk reduction;
◆ use active learning and participatory techniques;
◆ ensure that children and young people have a critical awareness of the messages that are portrayed in the media
(Health Development Agency 2001)

SRE includes the three interdependent elements of:

◆ knowledge;
◆ personal and social skills;
◆ attitudes and values (including emotions).

The elements of SRE

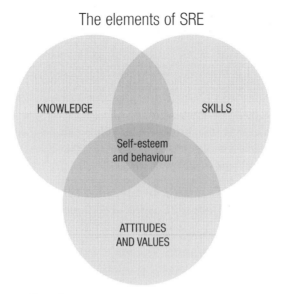

KNOWLEDGE

SKILLS

Self-esteem
and behaviour

ATTITUDES
AND VALUES

Active learning methods

Active learning methods provide a positive framework for enabling people to learn (Sex Education Forum 1997). These methods work by using creative processes to help acquire information, develop skills, explore values and form positive beliefs. We need personal and social skills to put knowledge into action and we need to practise using them.

Active learning can be an individual activity, such as undertaking research, but more often it implies working with others in groups whether this be a group of two people or more. Working in groups allows children and young people to practise skills, learn by observation, and build relationships.

The processes involved in active learning

Doing: Engaging in a structured activity – for example a problem solving exercise such as considering when would be the right time to have sex.

Sharing the experience: By working together to think about how different people might decide when the right time is to have sex. This might be in relation to specific circumstances, for example, religious beliefs, personal beliefs or expectations about there being trust, commitment and respect within the relationship first and when people are pressured into having sex.

Practising and testing what has been learnt: By critically working out what happened, as this young person did during an activity:

> **'It was really interesting that some people thought that the right time for sex was when they got married, and other**

> people thought that marriage was important later in life, but it was not important now, but it is important to know that there is respect and trust within the relationship. What I realised is that it is different for different people and I need to be sure that it is right for me based upon my own beliefs.'

Learning from the activity: Planning future behaviour, by working out what has been learnt and how that will change behaviour. For example, one young person explains: 'I realised that even though lots of people do have sex before marriage, I don't think I want to and that is ok.'

To be effective it is important that the young person is encouraged to reflect as part of the learning process. By asking questions such as the ones below, young people can be supported to think about how they can apply their learning to real life situations.

◆ What new information have I learnt?
◆ What new skills did I practise?
◆ What do I now think about…?
◆ How will I be able to use what I have learnt?
◆ What might stop me using what I have learnt?
◆ What else do I need to learn?

The benefits of active learning methods

Using active learning methods ensures that a range of faith and secular perspectives can be discussed within the process of learning. Views and opinions can be explored, rather than prescribed as fixed. Effective when used with groups of all ages and abilities, this type of learning also acknowledges that children and young people have many different starting points for their learning based on their levels of knowledge, background, experience and many other factors. We also know that a variety of learning experiences increases energy levels and interest, and that both children and young people and staff find them fun.

Core education skills are developed through active learning. They include:

Practical skills
◆ for everyday living
◆ for supporting others
◆ for future parenting

Communication skills
◆ listening to others' points of view, putting one's own point of view forward clearly and appropriately
◆ giving and receiving feedback

◆ handling and resolving conflict peacefully
◆ being assertive especially in pressured situations

Decision making skills
◆ for sensible choices made in the light of relevant information
◆ making moral judgements about what to do in actual situations and putting these judgements into practice
◆ acting responsibly as an individual or as a member of a variety of groups

Inter-personal skills
◆ for managing relationships confidently and effectively
◆ for developing as an effective group member

Problem solving skills
◆ for developing independence in thought and action and developing and defending values.

Including different perspectives and celebrating diversity

The Sex Education Forum's experience of working with teachers and other sex educators has shown that many shy away from including faith perspectives on issues such as marriage, homosexuality or contraception in case they frighten or exclude children and young people. Individuals with a faith do not all believe the same thing and there will be a diversity of views within and between religions.

It is important to include a range of both religious and secular perspectives, and to ensure that children and young people know about their legal rights. So for example, a lesson on contraception may include a variety of religious views including the Catholic belief that forbids contraception. Young people also need to know that they are legally able to access confidential contraception services and advice even if they are under sixteen.

The teacher has a responsibility to ensure that all children and young people feel supported and affirmed. For example, homosexuality is an issue where there is general disapproval from orthodox faith perspectives. A lesson covering this issue will need to ensure that children and young people know that homosexuality is legal, that the school upholds positive beliefs about diversity and that discrimination and prejudice is not acceptable. Colleagues involved in work for the SRE, Faith and Values Project described how homosexuality presents particular challenges towards the traditional understanding of sexual lifestyles and yet no faith condones bullying and harassment.

7: Linking to other areas of the curriculum

The National Healthy School Standard emphasises the importance of linking healthy schools activities across the different aspects of the curriculum, *'that links are made with other curriculum areas, for example science, technology, humanities and art'.* (*Guidance, NHSS 1999a*, page 13). For example, in English, young people could discuss the nature of relationships and values shown by characters in a play or book that they are reading, while in humanities, they could be discussing values and traditions belonging to different countries and cultures.

SRE within the broader Citizenship framework

Citizenship requires that pupils study, reflect upon and discuss topical moral, social and cultural issues. SRE is an integral part of the PSHE and Citizenship framework. Within the framework, children and young people could discuss a given topic on sex, sexuality or sexual health, in pairs or small groups before the group is brought together for a wider discussion. Alternatively, they could develop presentation skills by working in small groups to research a topic and then present their findings back to the group.

> ### Case study: Citizenship and shared values
>
> Bradford Interfaith Education Centre has worked with other countries to develop a number of school-based learning projects as part of Citizenship and learning about shared values. Some of the ideas and activities focus on relationships. A resource *Regarding Religion – Partnerships in education for Citizenship and Shared Values* (Bradford Education 1998) has been produced as a result of the work and gives ideas for PSHE and Citizenship

Citizenship also requires that pupils develop as active citizens. Pupils can be involved in the SRE policy development group, participate in or facilitate a survey or focus group on SRE.

Linking with religious education

Many aspects of sex and sexuality are covered within the Religious Education curriculum, and staff within these departments are a useful source of information and support as well as providing opportunities for collaboration.

The case study below highlights how one school has worked within the RE syllabus to explore the issues.

Case study: Religious education and sexual ethics at the Thomas Alleyne School

At the Thomas Alleyne School in Hertfordshire, the young people in Years 10 and 11 need to complete a paper Christian perspectives as part of their GCSE syllabus in RE. They look at a variety of moral issues, forming their own views and exploring how a Christian might respond to those same questions. Topics covered include those related to sexual ethics, for instance abortion, homosexuality, pornography, marriage and divorce. Other topics include IVF, adoption and care for people with AIDS.

A format for a typical topic/lesson might be:
◆ Asking the students to think about their opinions in relation to an issue.
◆ Facilitating a discussion on the issue ensuring that the complexity of the issue and range of perspectives is examined. Soap operas are always useful to stimulate ideas.
◆ Inviting the students to work out the traditional Christian stance.
◆ Looking at the biblical basis for the Christian stance.
◆ Exploring the range of different Christian perspectives.
◆ A small group role-play to discuss different views and opinions.
◆ Although the title of the paper is 'Christian Perspectives' and they must refer to Christianity, they can bring in other faith perspectives when they explore their own views. Members of the group who have different perspectives that are not Christian are invited to share it with the rest of the group.

8: Working in community settings

There are positive opportunities for developing sex and relationships education in the community, for instance through youth clubs, faith communities, young mother groups, and other locally run projects. Community settings can provide targeted approaches which meet the needs of particular communities or groups. They also offer young people a more flexible, informal setting than school for learning about sex and relationships. Another benefit is that they operate in real-life environments often in places where health compromising behaviour takes place. Hence SRE carried out in community settings can be successful in reaching marginalised young people who have slipped through mainstream SRE in schools and who do not access other services.

Case study: Training members of faith groups to become advisors to young people

Background

This new project is based in South East London which has one of the highest teenage conception rates in the country. In order to help reduce this rate, members from different local faith groups are being trained to act as a source of non-judgemental support and information to young people on sensitive subjects both within their faith groups and the wider community.

Process

Meetings took place with church leaders to gain their support and to help identify members of faith groups who might be able to contribute. Group sessions were organised with participants to explore topics such as sexuality, relationships and risk taking behaviour from young people's perspective. A group of people from ten faith groups have now been trained to support young people in their group on sexuality issues.

Issues and outcomes

The project workers needed to explain that the project is not seeking to put forward a particular view about sexuality and what is right or wrong, and is not representing the views of any one faith group. They achieved this by being clear about objectives and their roles purely as facilitators of the group.

The group faced some challenges about use of language regarding sexuality and other issues such as race. Skilled facilitation has been vital in ensuring that participants understand each other.

Gaining support of faith group leaders and ministers has been essential to the project's success. However, leaders in some groups, such as Islamic, Jewish and some Catholic groups, listened with interest but chose not to be involved. Project workers are keeping them informed of the project's progress.

The training process, facilitated by project workers, has been highly interactive and has led participants to consider their own values about sex and sexuality, and to think about how they communicate with young people. It has enabled them to develop greater understanding of the pressures on young people

---

and the role of sexuality in their lives. The process has also built their confidence in discussing issues which many may have considered too sensitive to discuss, such as homosexuality and sexual abuse.

The group is now planning the next phase of the project and is considering how to actively engage the young people in their faith groups, and thinking about the support they will need to help them do this.

Case study: the Guide Association

The Guide Association has developed a SRE programme in response to their survey, *Today's Girls, Tomorrow's Women* (2001). The survey, which explores the young women's key concerns, showed that relationships were a key aspect of their lives with which they felt in need of further help and support.

SRE is developed within the values framework of the Association and is part of their commitment to help girls and young women achieve their potential.

Many youth groups are run by churches or faith communities which aim to provide support and information about sexual and relationship matters for the young people attending.

Case study: Methodist guide to talking with young people

The Methodist Church has recognised that relationships are an important element of young people's lives and is a hotly discussed issue among their young people. They have developed a guide *Let's Explore* (2002) for church leaders to support them in talking with young people.

A range of projects have also been set up to target and support the particular needs of specific communities:

Case study: peer education with Bangladeshi young people

The NAZ Project works with a range of minority communities in London to support their sexual health. Working with Tower Hamlets local authority, NAZ developed a peer education project for Bangladeshi young people. The aim was to recruit and train young people to deliver peer education on topics including HIV, sexual health and relationships. A range of methods were used to develop their skills as peer educators, including role-play, video and visual resources. The young people were given vouchers as an incentive for becoming involved. The project was facilitated by workers from the same religious and cultural background as the young people they were targeting, and this was identified as an important factor in the success of the project.

Case study: Seventh-Day Adventists develop programme to support family life

The Seventh Day Adventists run programmes to support the family for those within their faith community. The aim of the programme is to affirm the importance of family and to provide nurturing and support for church members in relation to marriage, parenting and family living.

The Family Ministries Department offers information, training and counselling, as well as courses for married couples and those who are embarking on marriage. The courses are designed to develop communication skills, look at ways of handling conflict, and provide information about the support that the church gives. The programme also includes marriage retreats, family camps and lone parent camps. There is also a yearly conference and roadshow which features seminars and workshops on marriage, divorce, care, parenting, being single, grandparenting and being a teenager.

Section 3: Working with faith perspectives and particular topic areas

9: Major faiths and perspectives

This chapter gives an overview of the key values underpinning the major faiths as well as the Humanist movement. In addition, it provides each faith's ethical perspective on a series of nine topics. During the consultation process for this pack, these nine topics were identified as areas where educators felt particularly in need of guidance. They are:

- ◆ celibacy;
- ◆ contraception and emergency contraception;
- ◆ divorce;
- ◆ gender roles;
- ◆ HIV/AIDS;
- ◆ homosexuality;
- ◆ marriage and relationships;
- ◆ puberty;
- ◆ termination of pregnancy (abortion).

Suggested learning outcomes for each of these topics is provided in Chapter 10.

The Buddhist perspective

Overview

Buddhism teaches about moral conduct in life and society. It concentrates on virtue, peace, happiness, compassion and loving kindness as well as emphasising the importance of not taking advantage of others. The principles of impermanence, suffering and non-self or selflessness are the focus of contemplation in order to gain wisdom. This wisdom can enable those following the faith to let go of hindrances, enabling them to enjoy the blessing, 'may all beings be well and happy'.

Key topic areas

Celibacy

Ordained monks and nuns take the vow of celibacy to free themselves from the attachment of sexual desire and intimate relationships.

Contraception and emergency contraception

Contraception that prevents fertilisation is acceptable, as a conscious or sentient being has not yet taken form in the womb. While medically speaking, emergency contraception does not cause an abortion, a belief that conception occurs when the egg is fertilised (that is, before implantation), could make both forms of emergency contraception unacceptable.

Divorce

The concept of not doing harm to others would underpin the Buddhist perspective on divorce. Separation of a couple and the ending of a marriage should be carried out as skilfully as possible with the minimum of pain and the utmost sensitivity to each other's feelings.

Gender roles

Teachings of the Buddha proclaim that women and men are equal in their ability to reach enlightenment. Historically, women's arena was a domestic one; however, women sometimes followed a spiritual path. The Buddha said that nuns should not be made to perform domestic duties for monks, nor should monks take money donated to the nuns. Today, spiritual practices are open to women and men equally. In Theravada, both men and women can become Arahats (one worthy of reverence having attained the penultimate state of perfection), and in the Mahayana they can become advanced Bodhisattvas (those who attain this goal and return to help others).

HIV/AIDS

Buddhism recognises the need for compassion for those who suffer. Action that does not cause harm and is of benefit to others is demonstrated in Buddhist countries such as Thailand where monks and nuns offer care and support to those affected by the virus.

Homosexuality

Any actions that cause suffering are to be avoided. Analysing each situation in relation to sexual misconduct and causing harm will enable the individual to decide with the help of a teacher and possibly their Sangha (community/fellowship) whether the precept is being kept. Historically, homosexuality has been 'sporadically condemned as immoral in Southern and Northern Buddhism, but there has been no evidence of persecution for homosexual activities. An attitude of unenthusiastic toleration had existed. In China, there has been more moderate tolerance, and in Japan positive advocacy but I do not think this positive advocacy is found in Japan today.' (Harvey 2000, page 434)

Marriage and relationships
Many adult Buddhists are or have been married and it is considered an important social unit. Marriage, co-habitation and relationships that avoid sexual misconduct, can also be seen as a context for developing an understanding of the spiritual path. They can help to develop wisdom, loving kindness and compassion to support the attainment of enlightenment.

Puberty
The teachings of Buddhism are concerned with the ripening of the personality, which enables release from the ego-driven bonds of childhood that unchecked, may continue into adulthood. The physical growth of the infant towards adulthood may be paralleled with psychological, religious and spiritual growth. Puberty provides the bridge or developmental stage to engaging with an awareness of this 'inner training' on the path towards enlightenment.

Termination of pregnancy (abortion)
Consciousness does not die with the death of the body but continues its life without physical form. It will eventually be reincarnated into another living form. At the point of conception, consciousness enters the womb and human life begins. Terminating a pregnancy would therefore be seen as killing a sentient being. Other factors provide points for ethical discussion. They include the age of the embryo or foetus, risks to the mother or foetus, compassion for those who have had a termination of pregnancy and encouraging responsible and appropriate forms of contraception.

Core values underpinning these beliefs and codes of conduct includes those found in The Ten Perfections – the qualities that lead to Buddha-hood:	
Generosity	Patience
Good conduct/discipline	Honesty
Letting go/renunciation	Resolve
Wisdom/understanding	Loving kindness
Inner strength/energy	Equanimity

The Christian perspective

Overview

There are differing views among Christians on most issues about sex and relationships, including varied responses to education on these matters. The differences are determined by denominational allegiance as well as representing an individual Christian's personal response to and interpretation of their faith. Some take the view that sex and relationships education should be the preserve of parents and withdraw their children from provision even when carried out within a Christian or denominational values framework. Others adapt national guidance and curriculum advice to express their own community values. Many fully adopt the SRE programmes used throughout the educational system. Jesus' teaching of the fundamental Commandment, love of God and loving one's neighbour as oneself, provides the basis for core Christian values.

Key topic areas

Celibacy
Some Christians take a vow of celibacy as a way of expressing their commitment to God and the faith community.

Contraception and emergency contraception
For many Christians, as long as both partners agree, contraception is acceptable. For some there is a distinction between methods that prevent conception and fertilisation, and those that prevent implantation. This is based on the individual's understanding of when life begins. Some Christians, including the Roman Catholic Church, accept the principle of family planning but reject all forms of contraception that are considered artificial, only allowing natural family planning methods.

Divorce
While all Christians would subscribe to the belief that marriage is ideally a lifelong union, there are various attitudes towards separation, divorce, and the remarriage of divorced people in church. Some historic traditions in Christianity, e.g. Orthodox, allow divorce on the grounds of adultery as consistent with biblical teaching. Others, such as the Roman Catholic Church, respond to marital breakdown through a process of annulment – a formal declaration that a fully valid marriage, as understood by the Church, never existed. Christians in many denominations accept that divorce may be the only way forward where there is irretrievable breakdown in marriage.

Gender roles
Christian belief in gender equality is rooted in the biblical tradition that we are all unique, made in God's image and loved equally.

HIV/AIDS
Christian responses to people living with HIV/AIDS are based on compassion for all and a commitment to social justice, and not on a preoccupation with routes of infection. Many Christians are in the forefront of awareness-raising, education, care and support for those living with HIV/AIDS through faith-based initiatives, wider community organisations, hospice and health care provision, and overseas development work.

Homosexuality
There are opposing views among Christians on this topic. One perspective accepts the reality and diversity of sexual orientation but disapproves strongly of homosexual activity. Another affirms that permanent relationships characterised by love can be an appropriate and Christian way for lesbian, gay and bisexual people to express their sexuality. The expression of homosexuality is seen as wrong by many Christian denominations but the identity is viewed as neutral if celibacy is maintained. However, the issue is the subject of wide and developing debate among theologians of all major Christian denominations. (There is a Lesbian and Gay Christian Movement, see Appendix B.)

Marriage and relationships
Marriage is a lifelong public commitment before God and the community of faith. It is a holy state in which the couple's love for each other mirrors God's love for them. Christians believe that marriage provides the ideal context for sexual relationships and bringing up children, as well as providing mutual support, comfort and growth for the couple. Christian churches realise however that people fall short of the ideal and therefore forgiveness and reconciliation is available for those who seek it.

Puberty
There is no particular Christian rite of passage or doctrinal position relating to puberty.

Termination of pregnancy (abortion)
Christians recognise the emotional stress caused by an unplanned pregnancy, and some uphold a woman's right to informed choice. However, most Christians, in coming to a moral decision would raise questions such as:

◆ When does human life, made in God's image, begin?
◆ Is there a risk judgement to be made in respect of the life of a mother and/or child?
◆ Is a pre-diagnosed foetal disability so severe that viability would be compromised?
◆ What are the implications/consequences following rape?

Core values that underpin Christian beliefs include:

Love	Reconciliation
Respect	Integrity
Fulfilment	Hope
Justice	Trust
Forgiveness	

The Hindu perspective

Hinduism is a way of life as well as a religion. Having evolved over thousands of years, it is immensely diverse. A pragmatic religion with few orthodox views, it is a way of life providing codes of conduct by which individuals should live.

The concept of Izzat or honour is the same across Hinduism, Islam and Sikhism. It governs public behaviour, particularly about sex, gender, sexuality, marriage, relationships and sexual health. Diverging from prescribed codes of conduct may result in negative consequences such as rejection by family or community, including physical or verbal abuse at one extreme, and family and peer pressure to conform to religion and culture at the other.

Key topic areas

Celibacy

The four stages of life for a Hindu are: student, married householder, retirement and renunciation. A student will be expected to practise chastity until marriage. Marriage would traditionally take place after the completion of studies. Those renouncing worldly attachments may choose celibacy in pursuit of their spiritual goals.

Contraception and emergency contraception

All methods of contraception are permitted.

Divorce

Hindu law states that marriage is for life. Culturally, divorce may be practised, although it can be stigmatised.

Gender roles

Ancient Hindu law texts give men the dominant position over women in relation to religious activity and marriage. Although traditionally women tended to stay at home while men acted as the breadwinner, cultural change has meant that gender roles are changing and the division of labour is not so firmly defined. Legislation in India has abolished certain religious restrictions on women, such as widows being prohibited from remarrying. Sons are considered to be the providers of long-term security for the family.

In Western society, individuals tend to adopt lifestyles that suit their circumstances and are not tied to traditional gender roles.

HIV/AIDS
A karmic action conducted from a previous existence, is considered the cause of suffering, such as illness. The belief in the unity of creation and a responsibility for relieving suffering leads many Hindus to take action on behalf of those affected by HIV and AIDS.

Homosexuality
Lesbianism and male homosexuality is recognised in Hindu society and is considered publicly unacceptable.

Marriage and relationships
The basis for arranged marriage is around caste, faith and compatibility of family background. Love is not a prerequisite for marriage but is expected to develop afterwards. Marriage for a man is considered a sacrament (samskara). Traditionally the bride moves to the groom's family home and is expected to look after his family. Dowry was abolished by law in India but there may still be expectations of extensive 'wedding gifts'.

A marriage is considered to be between two families, not simply between the two people who get married. It is therefore important that the two families are happy with the suitability of the family.

Marriage is seen as an important role in life and it is considered unacceptable for somebody not to marry although reasons such as education may mean that individuals want to delay marriage.

Puberty
Puberty is not marked by any particular ceremonies for boys or girls. Behaviours such as dressing more modestly or less mixing with members of the opposite sex act as a marker for maturing identities. When a girl is menstruating she cannot take part in religious ceremonies or prayers.

Termination of pregnancy (abortion)
Termination of pregnancy tends to be disapproved of as all life is believed to be sacred. Religious views on this subject vary.

Core values that underpin Hindu beliefs include:	
Devotion	Faith
Respect	Honour
Duty	Commitment
Love	Obedience
Responsibility	

The Humanist perspective

Overview

Humanism is a secular philosophy. Its belief of respecting and benefiting others through shared humanity can inform clear ethical positions and strong moral codes of conduct based on individual analysis.

According to the Humanist philosophy, human beings have a potential value in themselves, and respect for this is the source of all other values and rights. This value is demonstrated by possession of powers to create and communicate in terms of language, human relations, the arts, science and institutions. These powers may be liberated by education, enabling men and women to exercise a degree of freedom in terms of the choices affecting their lives.

Key topic areas

Celibacy

Humanists are neutral about this. They do not celebrate denying oneself intimate relationships or harmless pleasures as virtuous, but neither would they condemn those who chose to be celibate.

Contraception and emergency contraception

Humanists do not believe that interfering with nature is in itself a bad thing, particularly if the consequences are good, so they do not believe that contraception is wrong. Indeed, in an over-crowded world many humanists see contraception and family planning as moral duties. If contraception results in every child being a wanted child, and in better, healthier lives for women, it must be a good thing. Humanists do not make a moral distinction between contraception and emergency contraception, though there may be practical and health differences that should be taken into account. No one should have a child until ready and able to take on the responsibility.

Divorce

Though marriage is a very useful social institution, humanists do not believe that it is 'sacred'. They recognise that some relationships fail, and so support liberal divorce laws. Divorce is seen as the best solution to some unhappy marriages, putting an end to quarrels and anger and improving the quality of life of everyone in the family.

Gender roles

Humanists support personal freedom. This must involve allowing everyone opportunities and choices in the worlds of education, employment and home. Neither women nor men should have restricted roles imposed on them, but neither should they feel they have to do everything. Within humanist organisations, men and women are treated equally.

HIV/AIDS and safer sex

Carelessness about other people's health and welfare is believed to be wrong, and people who know they have infectious illnesses, including those that are sexually transmitted, like gonorrhoea or HIV, have a duty to protect sexual partners from infection.

Humanists support full and frank sex education including the promotion of safer sex; how to say no to unsafe sex; access to condoms; proper funding for research and treatment, including help for poorer countries; and respect for the human rights of those with HIV or AIDS.

Homosexuality

Humanists do not think that any adult consensual relationship can be wrong in itself, and this includes homosexual relationships. If no one else is affected adversely and those involved take full responsibility for the consequences of their actions, there can be no good reason to condemn any sexual activity. Humanists oppose discrimination and prejudice against lesbians and gay men, and support changes to the law that would give them legal and social equality with heterosexuals. People should not confuse personal distaste for an activity with moral condemnation. Humanist celebrants offer non-religious ceremonies equivalent to a wedding in which gay couples can express their commitment to each other.

Marriage and relationships

Humanists support marriage as one form of stable relationship suitable for bringing up children, but think that this can also be achieved within a responsible co-habitation. They believe that it would be unreasonable to condemn any relationship that is freely entered into and does no harm, but think that there is a moral dimension to all relationships, including sexual ones and marriage. Hurting or exploiting other people is wrong, and this is always a possibility in a relationship. Unfaithfulness to a sexual partner can cause that partner great unhappiness, and can undermine the trust necessary in a loving relationship. Responsibilities towards dependants should always be taken into account.

Puberty

Humanists have no particular rituals to mark puberty.

Termination of pregnancy (abortion)

Abortion is not the best way of avoiding unwanted children, but as long as it is needed, most humanists agree that society should provide safe legal facilities. The alternatives, which would inevitably include illegal abortions, are far worse. Because humanists take happiness and suffering into consideration, they are more concerned with the quality of life than the right to life if the two come into conflict. Of course, all possible options should be explored and decisions should be informed. A woman needs to consider the long-term effects of abortion as well as the immediate ones. It is unlikely to be an easy decision and women should be supported in making their decision.

Humanism is the umbrella for a range of personal philosophies and therefore encompasses many values. The length of the list below reflects this.

The core values that underpin Humanist beliefs include:	
Potential	Love and affection
Acceptance	Caring
Commitment	Openness
Simplicity	Creativity
Spontaneity	Flexibility
Independence	Knowledge
Democracy	Trust
Individuality	Safety
Generosity	Protection
Sharing	Understanding
Respect	Balance
Unconditional positive regard	Enquiry
Empathy	

The Islamic perspective

Overview

Islam is a complete system covering all aspects of human activity including, religious, moral, ethical, social, sexual, economic and political spheres. Adherence to all the constituent parts of Islam is expected.

Key topic areas

Celibacy

Marriage is the state that should be aspired to and achieved by adults. Chastity should be maintained before marriage and fulfilling sexual relations are encouraged and expected within marriage. Celibacy has no meaningful place within adult life unless adults remain unmarried.

Contraception and emergency contraception

In special circumstances all forms of contraception would be permitted, for example, to protect the life of the mother, to prevent a pregnancy while the woman is breast-feeding, or for personal reasons dictated by conscience.

Divorce

Although divorce is discouraged, it is legal and permissible when the marriage has irretrievably broken down. After attempts at reconciliation, either party may call for the divorce. A waiting period (iddah) of at least three months must be observed before the divorce is finalised. The wife need not return the marriage gift (mahr) given to her by her husband at the time of their wedding. Both are free to remarry after divorce.

Gender roles

In Islam, men and women are deemed equal in both religious and social contexts. At the time of the Prophet (pbuh) women were given rights of inheritance, consent to marriage, rights to work and education, performing religious duties and protection from sexual harassment. There is an expectation that women will be appreciated for their character and not treated as sex objects. For some Muslim women, culture rather than religion may prevent these rights from being enjoyed.

HIV/AIDS

Life is considered a gift from Allah and it is therefore a duty for every Muslim to maintain a healthy body. Islam teaches the demonstration of love and compassion for anyone who is sick no matter how they acquired their illness.

Homosexuality

It is unacceptable and considered to be immoral. If actions occur in private, then it is between the individual and God, which will be decided on the Day of Judgement. If the action is public, then the upkeep of morality requires that punishment based on religious judgements may follow. As soon as a person turns back to God they can be treated with compassion and love. Sexual activity is celebrated only within marriage and is prohibited in any other state.

There is however a gay and lesbian Muslim movement called Al-fatiha: www.al-fatiha.org

Marriage and relationships

The contract of marriage outlines rights and responsibilities for both partners. Both sexes are considered equal and live in partnership but their roles are deemed to be different. Marriages are commonly arranged and love is expected to develop after the ceremony. A woman must agree to the marriage and cannot be forced. The husband often gives a mahr or marriage gift to the wife when they get married. Its purpose is to give the wife financial independence in the event of divorce. The Prophet allowed marriages between people of different status as long as their beliefs and values were compatible. Polygamy is permitted in some circumstances. Marriage is a source of support, companionship and comfort. It provides the environment in which to raise a family, the basis of the whole Islamic social structure. Sexual activity must bring equal fulfilment to both partners.

Puberty

When a boy reaches puberty, his parents must inform him that he has become fully accountable for his actions in the sight of God. He is expected to perform acts of worship in the same way as an adult. This will include praying five times a day and fasting during Ramadan. The physical manifestation of involuntary ejaculation could mark the point at which spiritual maturity will occur. The age of fourteen is usually given as the time at which parents have a responsibility to inform their son of his religious duties. There is no formal ceremony.

A girl of about nine is generally considered eligible to be spiritually mature. Her parents will inform her that she becomes accountable for her actions and must participate in acts of worship expected of all Muslims. Like a boy who has reached puberty, she will be expected to pray five times a day and fast at Ramadan. However, women are exempt from prayer and fasting during menstruation. The first sign of menstrual blood is a physical indicator of her change of status.

Termination of pregnancy (abortion)

Abortion is not considered acceptable unless the mother's life is endangered. Her life is considered to be more significant than that of the embryo if her life or health is put at risk by the pregnancy. In this situation her position in the family with its attendant responsibilities is more important than the potential of life residing within the embryo. This is the only circumstance where termination is lawful within Islam. A belief that the soul does not enter the foetus until the 120th day of gestation indicates that an abortion should be carried out before this time.

The core values underpinning Islamic beliefs include:	
Faith	Honour
Purity	Responsibility
Charity	Respect
Piety	Acceptance
Commitment	Self-discipline
Virtue	

The Jewish perspective

Family and community are at the heart of the Jewish way of life. Much of the religious observances are based around the home and family activities. There are close bonds between Jewish communities that help to maintain a global community.

Key topic areas

Celibacy

Chastity exists before marriage. Marriage is an important rite of passage in the faith's life experience. Deliberate celibacy is not seen as consistent with Jewish teachings, however those who remain celibate can still play an active part in the community.

Contraception and emergency contraception

No form of contraception would be acceptable without medical reason or guidance from a rabbi. Where the physical or psychological health of the mother is at risk if a pregnancy were to occur, then contraceptives can be used to preserve life and health. It is usually the woman who uses contraception.

Divorce

Jewish law does not recognise a civil divorce as terminating a religious marriage. Both the religious marriage and the civil marriage must end simultaneously. This is achieved by a divorce document (Get) that has to be written in addition to the civil divorce that both husband and wife must willingly agree to give and receive. In some circumstances representatives may stand in for partners. After divorce, remarriage is possible without any stigma attached.

Gender roles

Men and women are equal before God but traditionally have had a more complementary role in the 'unity' of their relationship.

The performance of religious duties from the Orthodox perspective falls mainly on the man, but women are able to perform most duties if they choose to do so, where appropriate. Traditionally women continue to be homemaker and mother, although these roles are beginning to adapt to the modern world in greater sharing of domestic responsibilities. In Orthodox communities, women are not permitted to participate in religious practices and certain domestic activities during menstruation.

The Reform and Liberal movements have extended equality to women in all aspects of Jewish life, including areas of religious function, such as women rabbis.

HIV/AIDS

According to Jewish law and custom, humans are 'created in the image of God'. Hence it is the duty of all Jews to maintain the health of the body. The Bible contains various examples of the treatment of illnesses and the curbing of epidemics. The tradition's respect for human life mandates that action be taken to prevent further spread of the disease. Alongside the laws for education and disease prevention, there is a duty of care and compassion for those who are ill.

Homosexuality

The Orthodox perspective forbids homosexual activity. However homosexuals should not be shunned or stigmatised in the community. Views among Reform and Liberal movements are more accepting of homosexuality. Judaism therefore forbids homophobic persecution.

Marriage and relationships

Traditionally young men and women are encouraged to marry early but today this primarily happens only in the very Orthodox community who generally use arranged marriages as a way of finding partners for their children. Because God created Man and Woman in the Garden of Eden, marriage is regarded as a state in which God has a special relationship with the two people involved. Marriage is seen as a mutual commitment between husband and wife, enabling them to value their own relationship and to bring up children. The married couple is considered complete. It is considered important for the community that Jews marry Jews. However, the faith line passes to the children through their mother. Within the Liberal Movement, the children of Jewish fathers are now regarded as Jews, but they would not be recognised as such by Orthodox communities.

In Orthodox communities, during menstruation, married couples will not engage in sexual intercourse or physical intimacy. Relations recommence after the woman has immersed herself in a Mikveh (a pool of water) especially constructed for this purpose.

Puberty

Boys' puberty is marked with a coming-of-age ceremony at age 13, when a young man legally becomes an adult, or 'son of the commandment' (bar mitzvah). In Orthodox communities the equivalent for a girl is at the age of 12 when they become bat mitzvah (daughter of the commandment) and are honoured in a special ceremony. In other branches of Judaism such ceremonies can be held up to the age of 18 or girls may be honoured in a similar ceremony, called a bat mitzvah. In Orthodox communities, once a girl has come of age, she is not permitted to participate in religious practices and certain domestic activities during menstruation.

Termination of pregnancy (abortion)

Termination of pregnancy is prohibited unless primarily the life of the mother is at risk or her health may be severely affected. In other circumstances, rabbinic guidance is sought as abortion is regarded as destroying life.

The core values underpinning Jewish beliefs include:	
Faith	Fidelity
Respect	Honesty
Devotion	Duty
Obedience	Truth
Justice	

The Sikh perspective

Overview

Religious and cultural beliefs and practices are closely linked. Sikhism shares some common beliefs with Hinduism as well as Islam and Christianity, and Sikhism itself has a wide range of identities. In the eyes of God and within the Sikh place of worship (Gudwara), everyone is equal. Even without official initiation, people still consider themselves a Sikh. Whether or not a Sikh conforms to the religious orthodoxy of initiation, they are often still aware of the roles and responsibilities of being a Sikh, and many people will accept the fundamental values.

In terms of cultural and social norms, family honour (Izzat), is emphasised. The notion of public and private behaviour impacts upon young people exploring their identity particularly on issues considered unacceptable such as sex before marriage and homosexuality. If private behaviour becomes public, then it will attract disapproval. Maintaining it in the private domain means that individual conscience will decide a course of action. The importance of collective identity means that public behaviour needs to conform to Sikh beliefs to maintain membership of the community.

Living within the faith in western society often requires compromise. While arranged marriage is important, marriage out of the community is growing. Young people are familiar with their legal rights and often use them to negotiate a love marriage, going to university or 'social mixing'.

In Sikhism there are five vices (immoral acts) that should be controlled as core discipline by all Sikhs:

◆ Kaam (lust)
◆ Krodh (extreme anger)
◆ Lobh (greed)

◆ Moh (worldly attachments)
◆ Ahankar (self-pride)

Ethics and morality are the basis of Sikhism, which are underpinned by the five Sikh institutions:

◆ Sri Gurn Granth Ji (The Sikhs Holy Scripture)
◆ Gurdwara (place of worship open to all)
◆ Langar (free community kitchen service)
◆ Gatka (the Sikh martial art)
◆ Anand Karaj (the Sikh wedding ceremony)

These are supported by six social, cultural codes of ethics:

◆ Democracy (Sadh Sangat) - community decisions by consensus
◆ Human rights - freedom of worship and divine self dignity
◆ Equality - between men and women and the eradication of castes
◆ Social Justice - ability to protect the rights of vulnerable people
◆ Freedom of Conscience - in mind and body (maan and tan)
◆ Service (seva) - voluntary service for the welfare of humanity.

Key topic areas

Celibacy
The ascetic celibate life is not considered a virtue. Marriage is the desired state for adults (Gristi Jeevan). Sex before marriage is prohibited.

Contraception and emergency contraception
Contraception is accepted as long as it is not seen as causing an abortion of the fertilised egg.

Divorce
Marriage is for life but divorce is permitted if the interventions of the family to reconcile the couple have failed. However, divorce is increasingly excluding the extended family and becoming a personal issue among couples. Reasons for divorce include insanity, desertion, cruelty, impotence, adultery or change of religion. Civil law is recognised as valid, and religious remarriage can be celebrated.

Gender roles
Sikhism advocates equality and the Gurus taught that women may perform any function and hold any office equally with men in the Sikh community. Culture rather than religion may cause difficulties for Sikh women attempting to achieve these teachings.

HIV/AIDS

The body is considered a temple created by God and should be respected and cared for. If infection occurs by breaking the code of discipline, for example through adultery or use of drugs, the individual may choose to exclude themselves from the congregation until they decide to commit themselves once more to the rules. Healing and caring are central teachings in Sikhism.

Homosexuality

While the Gurus did not mention homosexuality in their teachings, it is considered unacceptable because marriage, and sexual activity within this state, are the desired goal for adults.

Marriage and relationships

Marriage is a sacred undertaking and the expected goal of every adult. The family is perpetuated and extended via marriage and this fulfils God's wishes. Parents and the extended family will often be consulted in the choice of partner. Polygamy is permissible in rare circumstances, often where the first wife cannot have children, although it is rarely practiced today and is not legal in the UK. A man or a woman may fill the traditional role of head of the extended family.

Puberty

Sikh boys and girls may be initiated into their religious order, Khalsa, at puberty or when considered ready for the responsibilities of initiation. This means that they are formally introduced to the code of conduct that challenges injustice, promotes equality, high moral character and sexual morality. The ceremony of initiation (Amrit-Pahul) applies equally to young men and women. It is a mother's responsibility to inform her daughter of the physical changes during puberty; boys have no formal guidance but it can be sought from relatives.

Termination of pregnancy (abortion)

Abortion is considered morally wrong as life begins when the egg is fertilised by the sperm. However Sikhs also acknowledge the rights of parents and families to make their own decisions based on health grounds or situations where a rape may have taken place.

The core values underpinning Sikh beliefs include:	
Love	Equality
Faith	Justice
Acceptance	Commitment
Respect	Modesty
Strength	Chastity
Purity	Honour
Unity	Self-respect

10: Delivering SRE on particular topics

The previous chapter looked at faith perspectives on a range of topics which were highlighted during consultation as being areas which sex educators found particularly challenging. This chapter gives practical guidance on addressing those key topics within a classroom setting. It provides a general overview of each topic and suggests opportunities for learning about the topic within PSHE and Citizenship, taking into account different faith and cultural perspectives. The learning opportunities provided by each topic are divided into the three areas essential for good practice in SRE: knowledge, skills and attitudes.

Celibacy

> **'When a person over the legal age of consent lives without having sex (a person vows not to have sex and sticks by it!).'**
> ***NCB young member, aged 14***

Celibacy is often used mistakenly to describe a period of not having sex. 'I have been celibate for two weeks now' is a common saying which is really describing a situation where they have not had sex for two weeks. Celibacy means making an active choice to abstain from sexual intercourse for personal or religious reasons. It is not circumstantial.

Many faiths do not perceive celibacy as a positive choice, and some individuals may view it in a derogatory manner. There can be a misconception that celibacy is foisted onto the person owing to their inadequacies as opposed to it being something they might have chosen for themselves.

Learning about celibacy

Knowledge
◆ Understand the different religious teachings towards celibacy.
◆ Understand cultural beliefs about celibacy.

Skills
◆ Develop assertiveness skills.
◆ Develop communication skills.
◆ Develop skills of analysis.
◆ Develop the ability to resist peer pressure.
◆ Develop the ability to deal with negative judgements.

Attitudes
◆ Explore the range of attitudes towards celibacy.
◆ Think about and understand the right of individuals to be celibate.

Contraception and emergency contraception

> **'Young people know about the pill and condoms, but they do not have enough information about all the options available.'**
> ***NCB young member***

Contraception became freely available on the National Health Service in 1974. Its relative widespread availability has enabled people (primarily women) to manage their fertility and make decisions about the timing of childbirth and the size of their family. More recently, emergency contraception has provided a post-intercourse safeguard when other methods of contraception have not been used or have failed.

Young people's access to and use of contraception and emergency contraception has been the subject of wide debate on health, socio-economic and moral grounds. Education about hormonal contraception forms part of the Science National Curriculum Statutory Requirements at secondary level.

Despite fierce opposition from a few groups, young people (including those under 16 who meet legal criteria) are entitled to free, confidential advice, information and treatment.

In some faiths, the acceptability of contraception depends on whether fertilisation has occurred. In medical terms, fertilisation takes place when a fertilised egg implants in the womb. Some faith perspectives, however, believe that fertilisation occurs when the egg and sperm meet, and before implantation. As a result, they think that some current methods of contraception cause abortions. Those forms of contraception that cause excessive or irregular bleeding in the initial few months of use, could also pose problems for some faith communities, who prohibit sex during menstruation.

Learning about contraception and emergency contraception

Knowledge
◆ Know about the different forms of contraception and how they work.
◆ Know which forms of contraception protect against pregnancy and STIs.
◆ Understand emergency contraception (different sorts) – how it works, length of time, where it is available from.
◆ Understand how to access services.
◆ Know the law, and the age of consent for medical treatment and confidentiality.
◆ Know and understand the range of religious and cultural beliefs towards contraceptive use.

Skills
◆ Discuss contraception with a partner, health professional and parent or trusted adult.
◆ Negotiate contraceptive use with a partner.
◆ Skills of analysis to make informed decisions about contraception.
◆ Seek help and support about contraceptive choices.
◆ Use it properly (for example, taking the pill regularly, putting on a condom properly – when and how).

Attitudes
◆ Explore the range of attitudes towards contraceptive use and different methods of contraception (including natural family planning).
◆ Explore gender differences in expectations and understanding of responsibility.
◆ Explore the emotional and physical consequences of using or not using contraception.
◆ Explore what might help or hinder young people in accessing help and support services.

Divorce

> **'It [marriage] is a lifelong commitment and they should have taken it more seriously, but it is easier said than done.'**
> *Young woman, aged 16 (quoted in Sharpe 2001)*

> **'And my other friend when I found out his mum and dad had divorced, I said "oh right, that must be awful" and he said "no, its brilliant because they always used to argue before".'**
> *Young man (quoted in Sharpe 2001)*

Over the past few decades, the divorce rate in Britain has been rising and it is now at an all-time high. At the same time, there is an increasing social acceptance of divorce and possible remarriage. Any discussion of marriage needs to include divorce in order to ensure that the realities of the children and young people in the classroom are included.

Divorce is legal, and is becoming an increasingly accessible option. Within religious communities there are varying attitudes towards divorce.

Learning about divorce

Knowledge
◆ Understand the legal and civil rights in relation to divorce.
◆ Understand the social context associated with divorce and domestic violence.
◆ Understand the emotions associated with the experience of divorce.
◆ Understand the range of religious and secular viewpoints about divorce.

Skills
◆ Demonstrate empathy and offer support to individuals experiencing or affected by divorce.
◆ Able to ask for help and support if needed.

Attitudes
◆ Identify the range of feelings associated with divorce.
◆ Explore the different reasons that some people think are acceptable grounds for divorce.

Gender roles

> **'Boys are strong and girls are not.'**
> **Boy, aged 10**
>
> **'If boys have sex it's like wow what a stud and if a girl does everyone thinks she is a slag.'**
> **Young woman, aged 14**

Socio-economic changes in the post-war period have had a huge impact upon the roles of men and women in society. While these changes have led to increased education and career opportunities, women still remain largely responsible for the upbringing of children and the welfare of the family.

Within multi-cultural Britain these changes have occurred and yet their impact has varied depending upon the beliefs and realities of different social groups. In many faith communities, men and women have prescribed roles within the family. Many social commentators and practitioners believe that these roles are oppressive to women, but without understanding the thinking behind the division of these roles. Based upon these assumptions, some young women experience sex education as an attempt to save them from their faith and culture (Ray 2000).

It is important to look beyond these assumptions and recognise that many religious teachings demonstrate an ethic of *different but equal*, which may not always be exemplified in custom and practice.

Within British culture there are still strict rules of masculinity and femininity which boys and girls are expected to live up to (Biddulph and Blake 2001, Adams 2002). They need to be supported to broaden their understanding of gender roles and expectations so that they can achieve their full potential. Young people can experience a backlash from family, peers and communities if they do not conform to the ways that are expected of them (Adams 1997).

Learning about gender roles

Gender roles are primarily learnt by observation and socialisation and can be understood through discussion and planned exploration. Planned provision can provide children and young people with a forum where they can think about religious, cultural and societal expectations placed upon men and women.

Knowledge
◆ Recognise the range of traditional, religious, cultural and societal gender roles.
◆ Understand the reasons for and purposes of gendered roles.
◆ Understand the changing nature of gender roles.
◆ Understand the law in relation to gender.

Skills
◆ Develop a critical awareness of the messages they receive about gender.
◆ Able to recognise stereotypes.
◆ Able to discriminate against messages that are not relevant.
◆ Not being pressurised, influenced by stereotypical images of men and women.
◆ Develop a positive sense of identity and how to be in the world.
◆ Develop skills to manage the backlash when being unable to or choosing not to conform.

Attitudes
◆ Explore the diverse and changing roles of men and women in society.
◆ Think about the ways that people are treated if they do not conform to the conventional parameters.
◆ Think about the benefits of conforming to particular roles.

HIV/AIDS and safer sex

> **'I think that young people are aware of what safer sex means but feel unable to enforce it.'**
> **NCB young member**

In 1981, a new virus that we now know as Human Immunodeficiency Virus (HIV) was identified. HIV is transmitted through the exchange of bodily fluids. Although in the early stages of HIV there were some cases of transmission through blood transfusions that contained the virus, the primary routes of transmission have been through unprotected sexual contact, mother to baby transmission and the sharing of hypodermic needles. There is no cure for HIV and currently no vaccine.

There has been a significant increase in HIV infection rates among under 25s in the UK over recent years (PHLS 2000).

In industrialised countries there are treatments that enable people to maintain their health for longer. In developing countries, where these are not available owing to cost, more people are dying more quickly.

In response to the HIV epidemic there was a concerted effort led by the UK Government to promote safer sex (that is through condom use) as a strategy to prevent infection. The overriding value for many in relation to HIV and safer sex is the reduction of disease (Halstead 1998a). In contrast many religious traditions emphasise self-discipline which influences their approaches to teaching about HIV and safer sex.

Young people tell us that education about HIV does not provide them with the knowledge or skills that they need to protect themselves against HIV. As one young person said, *'I learnt more in one night from EastEnders than I did at school'* (National AIDS Trust 2000).

Within each religion and philosophy, there is a range of conflicting viewpoints about HIV and AIDS. The spectrum ranges from the notion of God's punishment for the sinner, if HIV has been acquired through sexual activity or illegal drug use, to support and care for those affected by the virus. Although this is a modern phenomenon, some members of faith groups make judgements based on unacceptable behaviours contravening prescribed codes of conduct. For others the underlying values of care and compassion override the notion of 'sin'.

Learning about HIV/AIDS and safer sex

In the UK, while anyone practising unsafe sex is potentially at risk of developing HIV, the virus disproportionately affects young gay men. Education therefore needs to be relevant to them without reinforcing stigma and prejudice. There is often a tendency to refer to 'gay sex' and 'straight sex'. This creates a false polarisation of sexual behaviour and risk. Clear and appropriate language helps to support an inclusive learning environment. Using terms such as 'partner' instead of 'girlfriend' or 'boyfriend' is inclusive and talking specifically about vaginal sex, anal sex and oral sex enables young people to understand sexual activity that is higher risk without stigmatising or stereotyping gay men's sexual behaviour.

Some children and young people will be living with HIV either because they are HIV infected themselves or because they live with someone who has the infection. Recent research (Lewis 2001) shows that children and young people living with HIV feel that education about HIV is irrelevant to them. Teachers either talk about HIV as a distant phenomenon or do not go into enough detail to help young people understand the emotional and physical issues relating to the infection.

'When HIV came up everyone was like "urgh" and I was just shrinking. I got up and left, got out of the classroom innit. I

didn't bother saying anything, because you know if you say something then it makes you look a little bit obvious. Like when people say to me "how comes you know so much about it?" I have to lie to them and say my mum works with children who have HIV, because I can't exactly say "oh because my mum's got HIV".'
Young woman, aged 16 (quoted in Lewis 2001)

Knowledge
◆ Know and understand the range of religious, societal and health perspectives on HIV and safer sex.
◆ Know and understand what HIV is and how it is transmitted.
◆ Know and understand what safer sex is, and how to protect yourself and a partner from HIV.

Skills
◆ Able to talk about, negotiate and practise safer sex.
◆ Able to access sexual health advice and services.
◆ Able to identify and manage risk.

Attitudes
◆ To explore prejudice and discrimination towards people living with HIV.
◆ To think about their attitudes and feelings towards risk-taking.
◆ To identify who they believe to be at risk from HIV and other STIs.
◆ To recognise how prejudice and discrimination can limit people's ability to accurately assess risk-taking behaviours.
◆ To think about how it would feel to access a sexual health service.

Homosexuality

'I think that schools should teach that homosexuality is a very real part of our society – there isn't enough education about this subject.'
NCB young member

Sex between men has been legal in the UK since 1967. In 2000, the Sexual Offences Amendment Act finally equalised the age of consent for gay men in England with that of heterosexuals (i.e. 16 years old). While arguably attitudes to homosexuality are becoming more accepting there remains a great deal of prejudice towards gay men and lesbians at social and cultural levels. Some of this is based on religious beliefs. Young men are more likely to express prejudice towards gay people than young women. (McGrellis and others 2000)

Young gay men and lesbians describe feeling invisible within classroom teaching, a common statement – *'I thought I was the only one'* – reflects their isolation. On the other hand, they also describe homophobic bullying and abuse at the hands of peers and adults which often goes unchallenged by teachers. There is emerging evidence that gay men and lesbians suffer from low self-esteem and increased vulnerability to mental health issues including risk of attempted and actual suicide.

Section 28 does not apply to schools and therefore does not prevent teaching about homosexuality. The SRE *Guidance* from the DfEE states clearly that *'all pupils whatever their developing sexuality need to feel that SRE is relevant to them and meets their needs'* (page 12).

Within many of the faith communities there have been struggles, tension, debate and dialogue about the acceptability of homosexual sexual activity. It conflicts with the traditional understanding of sexual lifestyles and while for some it is completely unacceptable, other faiths demonstrate greater acceptance.

Learning about homosexuality

Knowledge
◆ To understand the right of individuals to express their sexuality without fear of harm or abuse.
◆ Understand the law in relation to sexual activity.
◆ Understand the range of and reasons for religious and secular viewpoints on homosexuality.

Skills
◆ To challenge prejudice effectively.
◆ To express their own point of view.
◆ Listen to the views of others about sexual orientation.

Attitudes
◆ Think about the reasons why people are homophobic.
◆ Think about how it feels to be discriminated against.
◆ Value the right of individuals to live without fear of prejudice and discrimination.

Case study: Teaching about homosexuality in Catholic schools

Martin Pendergast has worked in a variety of Catholic schools on issues including homosexuality and homophobia. He is a member of the Teenage Pregnancy Unit's Independent Advisory Group.

Experience suggests that those delivering SRE in Catholic schools are often confused about Section 28. They are also often unclear about the Catholic Church's teaching on homosexuality and some basic principles of Catholic moral theology. Given the Church's historic vision of sexual activity as being confined to marriage, it makes a distinction between sexual orientation and expression. However, Vatican teaching now accepts the reality of sexual orientation, rather than viewing it as a perversion or sickness.

Approach

I have used two basic approaches in addressing homosexuality. One is to facilitate a group of teachers, by means of Inset days, to explore the issues themselves in a planned session. The other is to facilitate the session directly with students, using small group role-play, feedback, debriefing exercises and videos, followed by question and answer sessions. In one Catholic Sixth Form College in Telford, we used a story line from *EastEnders* when one of the characters was 'coming out' to his family. In groups of five, they role-played parents, siblings, and a young lesbian or gay person. After debriefing in small groups they shared the experience and raised questions in a general discussion.

The role-plays were entered into with great seriousness, not withstanding some initial tension and discomfort. There was a great sense of maturity among students and staff as they struggled with some of the issues raised. I came away with a feeling that this school was all that a healthy school should be.

Outcomes and findings

Support from the head teacher, governors and the community is vital for this type of work. Its success also relies on the students instigating the idea for the sessions, for example, using the story-line from *Eastenders* as a starting point. There is no excuse for homophobia within the Catholic community. Misuse of Section 28 and ignorance of denominational positions on homosexuality should not be used as excuses for not dealing with the issue. There is every reason to provide young people with the fullest information and education so that they can make informed choices about sexuality and relationships.

Marriage and relationships

> **'You only marry if you love somebody and nothing will change. If it's true love nothing will change.'**
> **(Suzanne, aged 14, quoted in Sharpe 2001)**

In the twenty-first century, marriage remains the foundation for family life and relationships across most of the major religions although there are many changes in both behaviour and attitudes to marriage. Marriage is also important to many people who are not religious, but who see it as a means of demonstrating public commitment to each other via either a civil or religious ceremony.

However the pattern of relationships continues to change. Couples generally get married when they are older. People often have a number of relationships before contemplating long-term commitment and many are choosing to co-habit rather than marry. Co-habitation is also often being used as a trial period before marriage. This appears to be part of the process of 'getting it right' for young people; not a process of moral decline, as is often assumed (Sharpe 2001).

> **'I'd want to get married rather than to have a long-term relationship, I'd want to have children in marriage so that's one of my quibbles if you see what I mean, I don't have any particularly strong views about sex before marriage, I don't know, again it is something that will happen to me if it happens.'**
> **(Edward, aged 16, quoted in Sharpe 2001)**

Children and young people are growing up within a wide variety of family groupings. They may grow up in married families, single parent families, foster families, unmarried families, or in reconstituted families with step-parents and step or half-brothers and sisters. Education about marriage and relationships needs to be mindful of these social changes and provide positive opportunities to explore the range of religious, moral and social views about marriage, relationships and co-habitation.

The recent RESPECT* study shows that children and young people want the opportunity to talk about the place of relationships in their lives now, as well as their hopes and expectations for the future. The findings from this research relating to young people's views on marriage and relationships are published in *More than Just a Piece of Paper* (Sharp 2001).

> One plus One, the marriage and relationships research organisation, is developing a range of exercises focusing on aspects of marriage and relationships. These will be available on their website in Autumn 2002, www.oneplusone.org.uk

Learning about marriage and relationships

Knowledge
- ◆ Understand the range of positive qualities necessary to form and maintain long-lasting and satisfying relationships, including trust, respect and honesty.
- ◆ Understand the legal framework for marriage and relationships.
- ◆ Explore a range of religious, secular and cultural perspectives on marriage.
- ◆ Explore a range of customs, ceremonies, rituals and practices.

*'Respect' (Youth Values: identity, diversity and social change) is a study of the moral landscapes of almost 2,000 young people growing up in contrasting areas of the UK. It was funded by the Economic and Social Research Council from 1996–9, on the programme Children 5–16 (Ref L12951020). For more information see www.sbu.ac.uk/fhss/ssrc/youth.shtml

Skills
◆ Develop a range of inter-personal skills such as communicating, sharing, compromise, negotiation.
◆ Develop empathy and accept mistakes.
◆ Able to identify the constructive and destructive elements of a relationship and being able to respond appropriately.

Attitudes
◆ Understand what they want from a relationship, and what they are willing and capable of offering while maintaining integrity.
◆ Explore gender roles and expectations in relationships, including the changing nature of gender roles in particular cultures and religions.
◆ Explore opinions about when to get married and the roles and responsibilities within marriage.
◆ Explore opinions about when they might get married.
◆ Think about how they feel about themselves as individuals within relationships.
◆ Consider the destructive and positive aspects of relationships, for example, being able to grow and develop within the relationship, being subject to and dealing with abuse, put downs and exploitation.

The Church of England, National Society has produced a web-based resource to support schools in educating children and young people in school about marriage. The resource offers an introduction that sets out the legal framework, the educational framework and rationale for teaching about marriage and long-term relationships and then offers four key strands through which to deliver the teaching from the foundation stage to post-16. The four strands are:

◆ commitment, faithfulness, promise, trust and security;
◆ friendship, companionship, nurture and comfort;
◆ children;
◆ sex/physical relationships.

The resource identifies the importance of acknowledging the diversity of children's experiences of relationships and marriage and emphasises the maintenance of classroom safety by ensuring that children are not asked to talk about their own experiences.

Copies of the resource can be obtained by visiting the website www.natsoc.org.uk

Puberty

> **'Girls have puberty, boys don't!'**
> *(Boy, aged 11)*
>
> **'Sex education is very important because that stage of your life
> – it's like very exciting but it's also – you get very frightened.'**
> *(Girl, aged 10)*

Children and young people tell us time and again that they still do not receive enough education about puberty. Many girls still begin menstruating without any knowledge or understanding of what it means either from the home, school or community (Prendergast 1994). The needs of boys in relation to puberty education are little understood and therefore often go unrecognised. There is increasing evidence that pubertal changes are beginning earlier in both boys and girls.

Retrospectively young people tell us that not enough attention is paid to helping them understand the physical or the emotional aspects of growing up (Sex Education Forum 2002). Girls report being bullied and teased for menstruating and boys are blamed for being insensitive. Without adequate education, children may move from childhood to adolescence feeling worried and confused about the changes that are happening to them. This can have a damaging effect on self-esteem and confidence.

Many different religious and cultural beliefs, customs and rituals are associated with puberty, for example, bar mitzvah, as well as a range of practices relating to the onset of menstruation.

Learning about puberty

It is important to consider how education about puberty is delivered. Single gender groups are more appropriate for teaching some groups of children. While girls need to know about their puberty changes such as menstruation and growth of breasts, it is equally important that the needs of boys are not ignored and that they receive education about the changes that happen to them such as voice breaking and wet dreams.

Knowledge
◆ Know and understand the emotional and physical changes relating to puberty.
◆ Know and understand who it is appropriate to ask for help or talk to about growing up.
◆ Know and understand the range of religious views, perspectives and practices relating to puberty (including menstruation).

Skills
◆ Able to ask for help and support.
◆ Able to demonstrate understanding and empathy towards others' experience of body changes and growing up.

Attitudes
◆ Think about who they would feel comfortable talking to and seeking advice from about growing up.
◆ Recognise and deal with feelings of embarrassment.
◆ Build confidence to ask questions.

Termination of pregnancy (abortion)

> **'They should know what the law says about abortion, where they should go for information and what different opinions of abortion are in society.'**
> *Young NCB member, aged 16*

Termination of pregnancy was first legalised in Britain with the 1967 Abortion Act. Before this Act, it was only legal for extreme medical reasons where there was risk of grave harm to the pregnant woman. Terminations are available on the NHS subject to legal requirements and local resources, and are also provided by some charitable organisations.

People have strongly held views and beliefs about termination. These may be based on religious doctrine but can also be attributed to a person's philosophical beliefs, or a combination of the two.

Learning about termination of pregnancy

Many resources advocate debating as a methodology for addressing the subject of termination of pregnancy. This focuses on whether it is right or wrong and forces young people to make an absolute decision. The Sex Education Forum believes that on its own this is not helpful as it prevents a more complex analysis of the moral, legal and medical issues surrounding the topic. It is important to offer young people the opportunity to know about termination and to understand the dilemmas. They should also develop the communication skills needed to discuss the subject with parents, carers, and health professionals as well as knowing how to access a termination if they want to do so.

Knowledge
- ◆ Know where and how to access advice, support and information.
- ◆ Understand abortion laws.
- ◆ Know that there are different methods of termination.
- ◆ Understand the range of religious and philosophical viewpoints about termination.

Skills
- ◆ Express their opinions and listen to and evaluate the views of others.
- ◆ Demonstrate empathy and respect for people with different views.

Attitudes
- ◆ Explore and identify different moral frameworks and understand how these impact upon choices.
- ◆ Develop an awareness of the messages about abortion that appear within the media and elsewhere in society.

Talk About Choice is a project run by Education For Choice. Workers visit schools to facilitate discussion of unplanned pregnancy and termination. For a talk with a large group, the emphasis is on disseminating information with plenty of time for questions and answers. In a group of 30 or under, it is possible for students to use the factual information as a basis for more in-depth discussion of termination as a social issue. It also gives them the opportunity to consider how to access appropriate advice and services to prevent, or cope with, an unplanned pregnancy. With the use of continuums, quizzes and structured discussion they are also able to explore the attitudes and values that will shape their decisions.

For further information contact Lisa Hallgarten, Education for Choice (efc@efc.org.uk)

Section 4: Reviewing and developing SRE policy and practice – an agenda for action

11: The step-by-step guide

This chapter outlines a step-by-step process that helps to review or develop sex and relationships education, both in terms of policy and practice. It provides an audit tool based on the criteria for the SRE themes within the National Healthy School Standard.

The criteria for the SRE theme are that:

◆ the school has a policy which is owned and implemented by all members of the school including young people and parents/carers and which is delivered in partnership with local health and support services;
◆ the school has a planned SRE programme (including information, social skills development and values clarification) which identifies learning outcomes, appropriate to the young people's age, ability, gender and level of maturity and which is based on needs assessment and a knowledge of vulnerable young people;
◆ staff have a sound basic knowledge of sex and relationships issues and are confident in their skills to teach sex education and discuss sex and relationships;
◆ staff have an understanding of the role of schools in contributing to the reduction of unwanted teenage conceptions and the promotion of sexual health.

The National Healthy School Standard identifies a number of additional criteria that relate to SRE, such as:

◆ equalities issues inform the development and implementation of activities;
◆ information is given on local support services for children and young people, such as sexual health and drug agencies;
◆ the whole school community (pupils, staff, parents, carers, governors and community partners) is invited to take part in policy development, physical, social and cultural activity and support each other's learning;
◆ the school openly addresses issues of emotional health and well-being by enabling pupils to understand what they are feeling and building their confidence to learn. (NHSS, 1999 pages 12, 14, 16)

A working group leads the development and review of SRE. Members of the working group might include: pupils, school nurse, health promotion staff, healthy schools coordinator, PSHE and RE advisory staff, faith group and community representatives, parents and carers, Connexions advisors.

The questions below can help in each stage in the development of SRE policy and practice.

Step 1: Identify how the development of SRE fits with other priorities
◆ How does it relate to LEA education development plans?
◆ How does it relate to local health priorities, for example, teenage pregnancy?
◆ How does it relate to school priorities? Should it form part of the school development plan?
◆ How does it fit within Healthy Schools work?
◆ How will it support marginalised and vulnerable children and young people, for example, those who are looked after?

Step 2: Review existing policy and practice
◆ How does the whole school ethos support a safe learning environment for SRE?
◆ What is the schools existing policy on SRE? How does it meet national requirements and non-statutory guidance? How does it take account of the differing needs of children and young people, for example, the needs of boys and girls and those with a faith?
◆ How does it fit within the context of emotional and social development opportunities offered within the school? How, when, where and by whom is it delivered?
◆ What is the content of SRE? Does it have clear learning outcomes addressing sex, sexuality, relationships, sexual health including faith and secular perspectives, social skills development and values clarification? How is children and young people's learning and progress monitored and assessed?
◆ How are multi-agency partnerships established and how do these different partners contribute and add value to SRE?

Step 3: Identify what the children, young people, parents, carers, the wider community and staff need and want from SRE
For all partners:
◆ What do these different partners need and want from SRE?
◆ What do they think of the existing programme? How do they think existing provision could be improved?

For staff involved in SRE:
◆ What aspects of SRE do staff feel confident in their knowledge and skills to deliver (include faith and secular perspectives)?
◆ How many staff members are trained to deliver SRE and what did the training consist of?
◆ What aspects are staff less confident with and what are their professional development needs? How will these needs be met?

Step 4: Identify local issues and trends
◆ What local issues need to be addressed within the programme, for example alcohol use and sexual risk-taking, racism and homophobia?
◆ Has locally available data been used to inform the SRE programme? For example, using school health profiling, teenage pregnancy data, school improvement data from the LEA, Connexions, Drug Action Team.

Step 5: Consultation and drafting policy
◆ Who will take responsibility for involving partners in the development of the SRE policy, including the values framework?
  ◇ How will children and young people feed into this process?
  ◇ How will parents and carers feed into the process?
  ◇ How will staff within the school, including learning support mentors, school nurses and the senior management team, feed into the process?
◆ How will consultation take place on the draft values framework and policy?

Step 6: Implementing and monitoring the policy
◆ How will the policy be disseminated to children and young people, parents, carers, the community and all staff?
◆ What are the professional development needs of staff? (Do staff understand the role of SRE in reducing teenage pregnancy and improving sexual health). How will professional development needs be met?
◆ Who will monitor the impact of the policy?
◆ When will it be reviewed?

12: Working together to develop the policy

This chapter focuses on working with partners in order to develop the policy. It gives guidance on making working agreements and provides activities which will help develop awareness of the issues.

Working agreements

Making an agreement of how people will work together helps a group to feel safe because participants get a shared sense of values and commitment to the issues being addressed.

Method

Ask the group participants to think about how they will behave with each other in order to discuss the issues.

Write up contributions on a flipchart and ensure clarity, shared understanding and agreement.

Ensure that the agreement is visible to all participants throughout the workshop.

Working agreement

Respect others' RIGHT to hold different opinions.
Try not to make assumptions.
Everyone has equal respect.
Try to enjoy listening, hearing, thinking and clarifying.
Do not use jargon.
Participate as fully as possible and support the participation of others.

Exercise 1: Sex and Relationships Education – Values, Rights and Responsibilities

This exercise is in two parts and can be undertaken as part of staff development in partnership with pupils. It could be carried out before engaging with parents, carers and the community or as part of the process of consultation.

Aim: To enable participants to develop awareness of all children and young people's entitlement to SRE and how this entitlement can be established.

Time: 60-90 minutes (Part 1: 30-45 minutes; Part 2: 30-45 minutes)

Method

Part 1
Divide into three small groups. Ask each of the groups to brainstorm one of the following and record on flipchart:
1. Rights and responsibilities of all children and young people in relation to SRE.
2. Rights and responsibilities of teachers, including the senior management team, in relation to SRE.
3. Rights and responsibilities of parents, governors and community members in relation to SRE.

Place the flipchart on the wall where everyone can see. Regroup into three different groups with representation from each of the three original groups. Ask the new groups the following questions.

◆ What similarities and differences are there on the lists?
◆ What themes, issues and patterns are developed in your discussions?
◆ What is the relationship between rights and responsibilities in SRE?

Each group gives a summary of their discussions to the wider group.

Part 2
Facilitate a discussion to develop:
◆ A charter outlining what children and young people need to learn about in SRE.
◆ An action plan to meet this charter within the school:
  ◇ Partnership with parents, carers and the community
  ◇ Participation of children and young people
  ◇ Curriculum development and breadth of opportunities
  ◇ Contribution of outside agencies.

Exercise 2: Developing a Values Framework

Aim: To agree a values framework for SRE.

Preparation: Photocopy handouts of 'Different views on why children and young people need SRE' (Appendix A) and 'Core values' (Appendix B).

Method

Part 1

Ask participants to get into small groups of 4-6. Hand out 'Different views on why children and young people need SRE' sheets. Ask them to discuss the aims and identify two or three that they think are important.

Part 2

Hand out the 'Core values' sheets. Describe how one or two core values relate to the aims of SRE.

In fours, ask the group to identify core values for SRE within the setting. Bring the whole group together to share core values and agree the ones which they feel should underpin a values framework.

Part 3

Explain how core values would look as a statement for a values framework.

In small groups look at the agreed core values and identify value statements that should underpin SRE.

Bring the whole group together to negotiate the agreed values statements for the framework.

Exercise 3: Exploring Perspectives On Key Topics

This exercise can be 'dipped into', and the structure used to focus on one topic in relation to a particular aspect of curriculum planning.

Aim: To explore the range of perspectives on different topics and identify the key learning outcomes for pupils.

Preparation: Familiarise yourself with Section 3 (pages 41-72) and use as photocopiable handouts where appropriate.

Method

Agree a topic or topics for discussion within small groups (examples include the nine topics covered in Section 3: celibacy, contraception, divorce, gender roles, HIV and safer sex, homosexuality, marriage, puberty and termination of pregnancy (abortion)).

Either on the photocopiable sheet or on flipchart paper:

1. Think about the different views, feelings, ideas, beliefs and myths about that particular topic for approximately 10 minutes.
2. As a team think about the issues this topic raises in terms of:

◆ planning of SRE;
◆ delivery of SRE (including outside visitors);
◆ professional development of staff.

Where necessary develop an action plan to address the issues raised by the exercise.

Further exercises focusing on anti-discriminatory practice are available on our website
www.ncb.org.uk/sef

Section 5: Appendices

Appendix A: Different views on why children and young people need SRE

◆ Learning the value of family life, marriage, and stable loving relationships.

◆ Encouraging young people to delay sexual activity.

◆ Developing self respect and an empathy for others.

◆ Learning about contraception and the range of local and national sexual health advice, contraception and support services.

◆ Only having sex within marriage.

◆ The avoidance of unplanned pregnancy.

◆ Safer sex and increased condom use.

◆ Learning the benefits of delaying sexual activity and the benefits to be gained from such a delay.

◆ Learning and understanding physical development at appropriate stages.

◆ Understanding human sexuality, reproduction, sexual health emotions and relationships.

◆ Learning the importance of values and individual conscience and moral considerations.

◆ Develop critical thinking as part of decision making.

◆ Learning how to recognise and avoid exploitation and abuse.

Appendix B: Core values and working definitions

Core values

When clarifying values during a consultation process it is useful to avoid the assumption that everyone attributes the same meaning to each value. Generally any discussion on values will be a mixture of highlighting and explaining a range of beliefs, attitudes and opinions. Clarifying cultural values, and putting them into context, can lead to highly emotional debates based on assumption. Listening to cultural values and aiming to extract core values and their definitions is often more constructive. It can build, rapport, trust and cooperation for a two-way learning process. Within this atmosphere there is a better chance of achieving an agreed values framework where everyone may feel heard and included.

In the list below core values are described with a minimum of social context: that is their great strength in providing common ground. It is not an exhaustive list and the values may be defined differently. However, explanation and agreement are the crucial factors.

Acceptance – To take as true. This could apply to any religious or philisophical doctrine or teachings

Altruism – To be unselfish, to work for the benefit of others

Attachment – To be bound by affection and loyalty

Awareness – To have a realisation based on knowledge

Belief – To have faith in the existence or value of something/someone

Bonding – A state of unity

Caring – To provide interest, protection, concern and affection

Celibacy – A reasoned decision to abstain from sexual activity

Chastity – A state of refraining from sexual activity with integrity and modesty

Choice – An identified preference made from recognised options

Commitment – A state of being involved and pledged to someone/something

Compassion – (i) Pure and unconditional love (ii) A wish that sentient beings be free from suffering (sacred meanings) (iii) Feelings of pity (secular meaning)

Confidence – A state of feeling certain about oneself, someone or something

Dignity – A calm state of seriousness, a sense of decorum, stateliness, formality and solemnity

Discernment – An ability to demonstrate sensitive understanding and to recognise and distinguish

Diversity – Variety, blend or multiplicity

Duty – A moral or legal obligation

Empowerment – A state of feeling enabled to act with confidence and authority

Equality – A condition where equal rights are enjoyed by all

Equity – A sense of fairness that recognises when different individual needs require appropriately different rights

Excitement – The arousal of an emotional reaction

Exploration – Research, investigation, analysis and study

Faith – A loyal and sincere trust and belief in something/someone

Faithfulness – Trustworthiness, fidelity, loyalty and being true to someone/something

Fidelity – Faithfulness and loyalty

Forgiveness – Letting go of anger or bitterness towards another

Freedom – A state of independence or being unrestricted

Fulfilment – A state where one is able to do what is required and enjoy satisfaction

Happiness – Contentment, delight, joyfulness, well-being

Honesty – A combination of trustworthiness, straightforwardness, honour, truthfulness

Honour – A combination of honesty, integrity, loyalty, being of good repute and sincerity

Humility – A modest perception and demonstration of one's own importance

Humour – An ability to perceive and enjoy being amused

Identity – What a person or thing is: distinctive character, individuality and uniqueness

Individuality – A sense of being separate, special, singular

Inquisitiveness – A state of eagerly seeking knowledge

Integrity – A combination of decency, honesty, goodness, incorruptibility, loyalty

Justice – Even-handedness, equity, fair play

Kindness – A demonstration of warmth, gentleness, understanding and consideration towards others

Knowledge – Information, facts, data: all that is known

Love – (i) Romantic attachment, sexual desire and passion (eros). (ii) Admiration, affection, fondness, tenderness, warmth for a close friend (philos) (iii) Unconditional love and compassion for all beings (agape) iv) Surrender of self through spiritual devotion

Mercy – A combination of clemency, generosity, forgiveness, humanity, sympathy and understanding

Mutuality – A state of dynamic interaction based on a balanced commitment and reciprocity

Non-exploitation – Recognising and proactively preventing ill-treatment, manipulation and unfairness

Nurturing – A responsibility for nourishing, caring for and rearing

Piety – Being devout in religion, reverential to God, sincerely spiritual

Pleasure – A combination of contentment, satisfaction and joy

Protection – To keep another from harm via guardianship or custody

Respect – Politeness and consideration arising from admiration and esteem for another

Responsibility – Being dependable, ethical, honest, diligent and accountable when in charge of someone/something

Rights – An entitlement to equitable and just treatment

Safety – Protection and immunity from risk

Self-determination – The free will to decide for oneself based on personal courage, dedication, will-power and single-mindedness

Self-discipline – A demonstration of self-restrained and self-controlled behaviour

Self-esteem – Self-respect and valuing

Sharing – A sense of cooperation, participation and giving

Trust – A firm belief and confidence in the reliability of something/someone else; to have faith in and be able to count on this expectation

Truth – A combination of accuracy, authenticity, integrity, reliability, validity

Understanding – A demonstration of insight, discernment, comprehension, wisdom and empathy

Unity – (i) A state of being one, in harmony and solidarity (ii) Being in agreement (iii) Being in rapport

Working definitions

The aim of this section is to provide some information on the distinctions between culture and religion, the sacred and the secular. This should help in addressing sensitive areas during the consultation process. The definitions are not answers to questions but should act as springboards for dialogue. As such it may be useful if they are explored in a spirit of openness.

Anti-discrimination – Anti-discrimination recognises inequalities and the direct and indirect nature of discrimination arising from them. It will actively challenge discrimination using the law, policies and guidance.

Beliefs – Acknowledge that a proposition is true without any tangible or scientific proof.

Circumcision: Male – The foreskin is removed soon after birth and has religious significance for many faith communities including Muslims and Jews. Culturally it is widespread in Asia and may be attributed to religious beliefs. From a health perspective it can be one response to penile cancer and circumcised males may have reduced risk of some STI transmission, notably HIV.

Circumcision: Female – See Female Genital Mutilation (FGM).

Culture – Culture is something alive and evolving and is concerned with how we behave together when part of a group with a recognised identity. It is generally something that we own, both sub-consciously and consciously, because we are aware of the cultural norms of the our chosen community, for instance we recognise that certain ways of thinking, behaving and talking are acceptable. Culture can rely on the majority of the group agreeing on how to behave with each other through work, leisure, art, education, food, language, religion, literature and so on. Set codes of conduct develop, based on values systems that are understood by those who are part of the culture. The group is aware of how history has influenced its culture. Leadership becomes important in maintaining codes of conduct and maintaining the culture. Within a multi-cultural society, dominant cultural norms can devalue difference by perceiving it as a threat, or by seeking to exclude by ignoring and making it invisible. Minority cultures may guard against assimilation and discrimination by creating very public and well-defined parameters.

Discrimination – Discrimination consists of actions that perpetuate the existence of social 'norms' usually formulated by the more powerful groups in society. It enables and supports the creation of stereotypes that limit the way that people are expected to think and behave. Discrimination treats assumptions about 'other' as facts and accepts these as the 'truth'. It often involves the exclusion of a variety of experiences, values and potential contributions from a wide range of groups and individuals.

Dowry – Traditionally and across many cultures, a dowry represents a daughter's inheritance from her father. In cultures where inheritance of family estates passes to the eldest male, the custom of giving a dowry to the groom's parents, upon marriage of a daughter, is seen as an essential part of the arrangement. The practice is different in Islam where the groom gives his bride a dowry at their wedding, to ensure her financial security. In countries where the custom of women bringing dowries to their husband's family is strong, the birth of a girl child may be seen as a long-term drain on limited or non-existent resources.

Equal Opportunities – Equal Opportunities legislate against discrimination and promote the notion of equal rights for all. More recently the notion of Equity has superseded equal opportunities with its focus on recognising individual circumstances of inequality and formulating appropriate interventions to create an equalised starting point.

Faith – Belief in philosophical doctrines that may underpin religious or secular ideologies.

Female Genital Mutilation – There are three forms of female genital mutilation: (i) the circumferential excision of the clitoral prepuce, (ii) excision of the prepuce and removal of the gland of the clitoris or (iii) the whole of the clitoris itself and infibulation, consisting of excision and joining of the two sides of the vulva, stitching with silk thread or catgut, or with thorns. A small posterior opening is left to allow the exit of urine and menstrual blood.
There is no religious significance to FGM. The intention of family members, mainly mothers, grandmothers and female relatives, is not one of abuse but stems from strongly held cultural beliefs that the practice of FGM will be of long-term benefit to the child or adolescent girl.
In Britain the Female Circumcision Act of 1986 prohibits anyone, medical staff or traditional midwives, from carrying out this practice. Issues concerning re-infibulation after childbirth require a series of dialogues between women in relevant communities, women and their husbands, women and health care professionals, and in some cases, where child protection is an issue, families and social services. Taking a female child to another country for FGM is a recognised child protection issue.

Hijab – This usually involves Muslim women covering their arms to the wrist and legs to the ankles as well as covering their heads with a scarf or veil. It demonstrates modest behaviour through dress. Many Islamic women consider this dress code to be liberating, as they can actively engage in society without attracting sexual harassment.

Izzat – The concept of maintaining family honour through acceptable behaviour.

Mahr – A marriage gift given to the wife by the husband on the occasion of their marriage. Its purpose is to give the wife financial independence in the event of divorce.

Marriage (Arranged) – Extended families and parents seek out compatible potential spouses for their children. Religious beliefs, education, status, common interests, etc., may all be factors that initiate the process of two people meeting and making choices. An arranged marriage allows either party to consent or decline the match.

Marriage (Forced) – Women are not allowed to say no to a match made by their family and are coerced into the marriage.

Monogamy – The practice of being married to only one person at a time. Socially, this definition often extends to sexual relationships outside marriage in terms of sexual fidelity.

Morality – Principles concerned with defining right and wrong conduct which could be in both a relative and absolute manner.

Natural Family Planning – This contraceptive method is based on the naturally occurring signs of ovulation which identifies the fertile and infertile phases of the menstrual cycle in order to prevent or plan a pregnancy. Some faiths, including the Catholic Church, only allow natural family planning, rejecting all other forms of contraception because they are artificial.

Philosophy – The study of the structures of thought that shape individual and collective views of the world. Generally this gets categorised in areas such as Epistemology – questions about knowledge; Metaphysics – time, space; God – cause and reality; Ethics – good and bad; Aesthetics – art and beauty; and Political Philosophy.

Polyandry – The practice of a woman having more than one husband. This is seen as unacceptable by most religions and many cultures. The right of the child to know its father is the rationale behind this prohibition.

Polygamy – The practice of a man having more than one wife or a woman having more than one husband.

Polygyny – The practice of a man having more than one wife. Strict codes of equality for all wives regarding physical and emotional needs are expected by religions such as Islam who allow but do not necessarily encourage this practice.

Purdah – The seclusion of women from men in terms of living separately and by means of being completely veiled in public. Historically it was a practice used by Hindus, Persians and some Christians.

Religion – An attitude of awe towards God or gods, the spiritual or the mystery of life. Belief and worship based on shared values accompanies this faith. Religion and culture may be interwoven but are separate things. Religion may specify particular codes of conduct, practices, beliefs and attitudes yet cultural traditions and customs can overrule religious statements and beliefs.

Secular – A movement away from religious thought and doctrines sometimes described as the desacralisation of the world and its institutions.

Suffering – In a religious sense suffering may be seen as the result of immature free will, evil, karma or delusion. Suffering can provide a vehicle to recognise and choose a particular path based on a specific faith. This path would aim to conquer or transcend this state by living a chosen faith, could bring closeness to unity with God or a sense of fulfilment, liberation or enlightenment.

Values – Describe what is considered of great worth and what is highly prized. They will consciously or unconsciously underpin a range of philosophies and belief systems.

Valuing diversity – 'Diversity' is a concept that recognises the benefits to be gained from difference. Valuing diversity seeks to include and involve groups and individuals from many sections of society rather than the more powerful few. By accepting the strengths present in diversity, it aims to utilise these proactively and positively for the benefit of all.

Appendix C: Useful organisations

If you want further information about local and national religious groupings and organisations please contact:

Sex Education Forum
8 Wakley Street
London
EC1V 7QE

Tel: 020 7843 6056
Fax: 020 7843 6053
www.ncb.org.uk/sef
E-mail: info@sexedforum.ncb.org.uk

Interfaith Network
5-7 Tavistock Place
London
WC14 9SW

Tel: 020 7388 0080
www.interfaith.org.uk

The following organisations are members of the Sex Education Forum.

Organisation	Web address
ACET	www.acetuk.org
APAUSE	www.ex.ac.uk/sshs/apause
Association for Health Education Co-ordinators (ASHEC)	Not available
AVERT	www.avert.org.uk
Barnardos	www.barnardos.org.uk
Black Health Agency (BHA)	Blackhealthagency.org.uk (under construction)
British Humanist Association	www.humanism.org.uk
Brook Advisory Centres	www.brook.org.uk
Catholic Education Service	www.catholiceducation.org.uk
Centre for HIV and Sexual Health	www.sexualhealthsheffield.co.uk
Childline	www.childline.org.uk
The Children's Society	www.the-childrens-society.org.uk
Church of England Board of Education	www.natsoc.org.uk
Community Practitioners and Health Visitors Association (CPHVA)	www.msfcphva.org
Education for Choice	www.efc.org.uk
Families and Friends of Lesbians and Gays (FFLAG)	www.fflag.org.uk
Forward	www.forward@dircon.co.uk
fpa	www.fpa.org.uk
Girlguiding UK	www.guides.org.uk
Image in Action	Not available
Jewish Marriage Council	www.jmc-uk.org

League of Jewish Women	Not available
Lesbian and Gay Christian Movement (LGCM)	www.lgcm.org.uk
Marriage Care	www.marriage.org.uk
Medical Foundation for AIDS and Sexual Health	www.medfash.org.uk
MENCAP	www.mencap.org.uk
The Methodist Church	www.methodist.org.uk
The Mother's Union	www.themothersunion.org.uk
National AIDS Trust (NAT)	www.nat.org.uk
National Association for Governors and Managers (NAGME)	www.nagme.org.uk
National Association for Pastoral Care in Education (NAPCE)	www.warwick.ac.uk/wie/napce
National Children's Bureau (NCB)	www.ncb.org.uk
National Council of Women of Great Britain	www.ncqgb.org.uk
National Health Education Group (NHEG)	www.nheg.org.uk
National Society for the Prevention of Cruelty to Children (NSPCC)	www.nspcc.org.uk
National Youth Agency	www.nya.org.uk
NAZ Project London	www.naz.org.uk
NCH	www.nch.org.uk
NSCOPSE	Not available
One Plus One	www.oneplusone.org.uk
Parenting Education and Support Forum	www.parenting-forum.org.uk
RELATE	www.relate.org.uk
Royal College of Nursing	www.rcn.org.uk
Save the Children Fund	www.savethechildren.org.uk
Society for Health Promotion Officers and Personal Relationships of People with a Disability	www.spod-uk.org.uk
Society of Health Advisors in STD (SHASTD)	www.shastd.org.uk
TACADE	www.tacade.com
Terrence Higgins Trust	www.tht.org.uk
Trust for the Study of Adolescence (TSA)	www.tsa.uk.com
Working With Men	www.workingwithmen.org
YWCA	www.ywca-gb.org.uk

Appendix D: References

Adams, J (1997) *Girlpower: How far does it go? A resource and training pack on self-esteem for girls and young women*. Sheffield Centre for HIV and Sexual Health

Adams, J (2002) *Go Girls: Supporting emotional development and building self-esteem*. Centre for HIV and Sexual Health

Biddulph, M and Blake, S (2001) *Moving Goalposts: Setting a training agenda for sexual health work with boys and young men*. Family Planning Association

Blake, S and Frances, G (2001) *Just Say No! to Abstinence Education – a report of a sex education study tour to the United States*. Sex Education Forum

Bradford Education (1998) *Regarding Religion – Partnerships in education for Citizenship and Shared Values*. Bradford Education

Carrera, C and Ingham, R (1998) 'Liaison between parents and schools on sex education policies – identifying some gaps', *Sex Education Matters 15, pp. 3-4*

Department of Education and Employment (2000) *Sex and Relationship Education Guidance* (0116/2000). HMSO. Obtainable by e-mailing dfee@prologistics.co.uk and quoting ref 0116/2000.

Guide Association (2001) *Today's Girl, Tomorrow's Women*. Guide Association

Halstead, J M (1998a) 'Developing a values framework for sex education in a pluralist society', *Journal of Moral Education*

Halstead, J M 'Values and sex education in a multi-cultural society' *in* Reiss, M and Abdul Mabud, S (1998b) *Sex Education and Religion*. The Islamic Academy

Harvey, P (2000) *An Introduction to Buddhist Ethics*. Cambridge University Press

Health Development Agency (2001) *Characteristics of effective interventions designed to reduce teenage pregnancy – An update*. Health Development Agency

Lenderyou, G and Porter, M (1994) *Sex Education, Values and Morality*. Health Education Authority

Lewis, E (2001) *Afraid to Say: The needs and views of young people living with HIV/AIDS*. Strutton Housing and National Children's Bureau

McGrellis and others (2000) *Through the Moral Maze – a quantitative study of young people's values*. The Tuffnell Press

National AIDS Trust (2000) 'I learnt more from EastEnders in one night than I did at school.' Report of young people's consultations on HIV. National AIDS Trust

National Foundation for Educational Research/Health Education Authority (1994) *Parents, Schools and Sex Education*. Health Education Authority

National Healthy School Standard (1999a) *Guidance*. Department of Health/Department for Education and Skills. This document and *Getting started* (see below) are available by visiting the Wired for Health website – wiredforhealth.gov.uk – or by contacting 020 7430 0850.

National Healthy School Standard (1999b) *Getting Started*. Department of Health/ Department for Education and Skills

National Healthy School Standard (2001) *SRE Support Materials*. Department of Health/Department for Education and Skills

North West Lancashire Health Promotion Unit *Mazhab and Sexuality (Faith and Sexuality). A discussion paper on sexual health for community workers from four faith perspectives.* Lancashire Health Promotion Unit

OfSTED (2002) *Sex and Relationships*. OfSTED

Prendergast, S (1994) *This is the Time to Grow Up – Girls' experiences of menstruation*. Family Planning Association

Public Health Laboratory Services (2000)

QCA/DfEE (1999) *National Curriculum Handbook for Secondary School Teachers*. QCA/DfEE

Ray, C (2000) *Forum Factsheet 21 – Meeting the needs of girls and young women in sex and relationships education*. Sex Education Forum

Robin, A, Singh, G and Thompson, H (1995) *Rishtae aur Zimmervarian – Relationships and responsibility: sexual health programme with BME communities. A report*. North West Lancashire Health Promotion Unit

Sarwar, G (1996) *Sex Education – the Muslim Perspective*. The Muslim Educational Trust

Scott, L (1996) *Partnership with Parents – a guide for schools and those working with them*. Sex Education Forum

Sex Education Forum (1997) *Forum Factsheet 12. Effective Learning: Approaches to teaching sex education*. Sex Education Forum

Sex Education Forum (1999) *The Framework for Sex and Relationships Education*. Sex Education Forum

Sex Education Forum (2000) *Our Charter for Effective Sex and Relationships Education*. Sex Education Forum

Sex Education Forum (2002) *Sex and Relationships, Myths and Education – young people talking on video*. Sex Education Forum

Sharpe, S (2001) *More than Just a Piece of Paper: Young people's views on marriage and relationships*. National Children's Bureau

Smart, N (1989) *The World's Religions*. Cambridge University Press

Social Exclusion Unit (1999) Teenage Pregnancy. HMSO

The Methodist Church (2002) *Let's Explore*. Methodist Church

Thomson, R (ed.) (1993) *Religion, Ethnicity and Sex Education: Exploring the Issues*. Sex Education Forum

Thomson, R, and Scott, L (1992) *An Enquiry into School Sex Education*. Sex Education Forum

Index